I0037888

"Going Broke is No Joke! is a fascinating, eye ɹ ᵤ
offers some of the best, practical, no-nonsense advice on managing your money that I have ever seen. It is a 'must read' for
people of all ages. My students will love it!

—Mozella Perry Ademiluyi, Wealth Literacy Educator

"I am always amazed at the depth of knowledge Patricia Davis
has when it comes to money matters. What's even more impres-
sive is how much of it she can pack into such a small space and
have her readers come out the other side with so much more
knowledge than they had at the outset. As was the case with
her other two books, this one, too, is chock-full of information
that will stand anyone in good stead for years to come. I love
this book!"

—Kathleen Henschel, Retired Financial Executive

"Patricia Davis has taught numerous classes to members of our
credit union, and, she is one of our most-requested educators.
Now, she has put some of her vast knowledge into a form that
many can read, enjoy, and use to become more informed about
the rules of the money game. *Going Broke is No Joke!* is packed
with solid tips on a wide range of financial topics such as banking, budgeting, credit, student loans, and job loss. It is truly
worth the price."

—Cheryl Pyle, Credit Union Executive

"Have you ever fantasized about what life would be like if you
had no money worries? In *Going Broke is No Joke!,* Patricia Davis
offers great advice on how to take charge of all aspects of your
financial life so you can be better informed, more relaxed, and
less fearful. It is the perfect book for these challenging times."

—Skip Bennett, Financial Advisor

"Without a doubt, Patricia Davis is the reason I have an orderly, well-planned out financial life. She now has put some of those tips she shared with me into a new book, *Going Broke is No Joke!*, so that you, too, can make smart, savvy decisions about your money. I heartily recommend that you pick up a copy. You'll be glad you did!"

—Mischelle Johnson, Retired Educator

"As with her earlier books, I was again privileged to read the early drafts of *Going Broke is No Joke!*. It is a must read for anyone who wants to understand the basic rules of the money game and wants to play it to win. Davis lays out, very clearly, "52 money tips everybody should know" to help put themselves on a sure footing to a solid financial future."

—Lee Straus, Family Financial Advisor

"The bad guys must hate Patricia Davis, for in her chapter on scams, she unveils enough of their dirty secrets to practically put them out of business. The information she reveals and the warnings she gives will certainly cause you to think twice before giving your money to any stranger. That part alone makes this book worth the money."

—Eric Johnson, Retired Circuit Court Judge

Going Broke is No Joke!

52 Money Tips Everybody Should Know

Patricia A. Davis M.B.A., M.S.

Going Broke is No Joke!
52 Money Tips Everybody Should Know

Copyright @2017 by Patricia A. Davis, M.B.A., M.S.

Published by Your Money Wiz Publishers
Cover and interior design by Constellation Book Services

ISBN 978-0-9827037-9-3
eISBN: 978-09827037-3-1

All rights reserved. No part of this book may be reproduced or transmitted in any form or by any means without written permission from the author.

Going Broke is No Joke! provides responses to 52 money-related issues faced by many. The author is not rendering specific legal or financial advice, and recommends that you seek out such prior to implementing any suggestions made in this book.

Printed in the United States of America

DEDICATION

*To my husband, Jim Davis,
whose encouragement and support
helped make this book a reality*

Contents

.

Acknowledgements

The stories, the ideas and the strategies shared in *Going Broke is No Joke!* are not mine alone. The book has come together through the help of many friends, relatives and colleagues. To each of you who has played a part, I say a heartfelt thank you. You have all contributed to the contents of this book.

In particular, I am especially grateful to these talented, patient and creative individuals for their guidance and support:

- My husband, **Jim Davis,** who believed in me and my ability to write a third book, encouraged me, let me know when I needed to start over (I hated that part!), and helped with research when I was too involved to do it myself. Jim's edits, re-reads and critical comments improved this book 100 percent.

- My very close friends **Annette Ferrell, Kathy Henschel,** and **Lee Straus,** who, once again, gave their time, energy, and knowledge to make *Going Broke is No Joke!* more accurate, easier to follow and the responses more succinct.

- Certified Credit Counselor, Radio Talk Show Host and good friend, **Chris Bridges,** whose experience as a credit coach and vast knowledge about all things credit were evident as we co-authored Chapter 4. I thought I knew a lot about credit. Perhaps I do, but, Chris knows more.

- **Martha Bullen,** my Quantum Leap book marketing coach, who steered me along every step of this journey. Martha provided immeasurable guidance on every aspect

of the book — title, organization and structure, cover de-
signs, book launch plan, publishing platforms and book
review team.

▸ **Christy Collins,** who took my manuscript and so artfully
turned it into a book with beautifully designed front and
back covers, and an attractive interior layout.

▸ **Jennifer Matthews,** my friend — a veteran author her-
self — whose pointed questions caused me to rethink the
entire concept of the book and the presentation of the
money tips.

▸ **Margaret E. Steele,** my editor, whose eagle eye seemed
to catch every extra comma, missing period and cumber-
some or inconsistent sentence.

Finally, thanks to those of you who will take the time to read
Going Broke is No Joke! to enhance your own knowledge of personal finance and the rules of the money game. I hope these 52
money tips will both ease and hasten your journey on the road to
financial freedom.

Why I Wrote This Book

My own story started many years ago. I was born the fourth of five children into a two-parent home. We lost our father when I was just 14 years old. My siblings and I were fortunate (though we didn't think so at the time) to have been born to a smart woman (Mimi, as she came to be affectionately called) who understood the money game, knew how to play it, and was determined to teach her children its rules and to make us live by them.

At the time, we thought Mimi was mean, stingy, and just didn't want to give us what we asked for. Little did we understand that 1) she didn't have enough money to give us everything we wanted; 2) she was working diligently to stretch the money she did have; and 3) she was determined to teach us lessons to last a lifetime. She said, "The time will come when you will appreciate what I am trying to teach you." She was right! We have come to value her teachings greatly, and they have stood us all in good stead.

My earliest recollection of anything having to do with money goes back to when I was a little girl—just five years old. I saw what looked like a lot of change on my mother's dresser and helped myself to a nickel since I didn't think she would miss it. I didn't realize that she had just gotten change for a dollar; she knew exactly how much she had on that dresser; and she and I were the only two people in the house. When she noticed that a nickel was missing, it pointed to only one person—me—and I got the spanking of my life! Boy, did I learn a lesson! Mimi threatened to put me in reform school (a place for bad children back then), and I was scared to death. I learned that lesson well and never touched another cent of hers.

That incident happened many decades ago, and I still remember it as though it were yesterday. There was no Judge Judy or Judge Greg Mathis to resolve money matters. We had our own judge, "Mimi Staunton." She was both our judge and jury. We were taught that you did not touch things that did not belong to you; you returned anything you borrowed; a loan is a loan, it is not a gift; and a whole host of other lessons, including how to respect money, and to have money, you had to work for it. My siblings and I have passed her teachings down generations.

Later in life, I came to realize a lot of people, both old and young, were not so lucky as to have learned some of the money (and life) lessons Mimi taught us. Because I have been guided by these rules and have witnessed the consequences of doing just the opposite, helping others learn money skills has become my passion—my life's work. I study it, talk about it, read about it, and write about money constantly.

My spouse, Jim Davis, and I were fortunate to both have parents who gave us a strong foundation in money management, not in environments where money was abundant, but in poor households where our parents lived from paycheck to paycheck and struggled to make ends meet. In our respective households, we observed and absorbed concepts that later formed the foundation of how we have managed our money, at first, a very small amount, up to today, where, thankfully, we have substantially more. (We had $600 between us when we married.)

It hasn't all been easy. There have been setbacks—job loss, illness, injuries,—but, by applying our guiding principles and some luck, we came through each one financially stronger. Those principles did not come to us in a neat, spiral-bound notebook or a framed plaque to hang on a wall. Beginning with our first year of marriage, we read everything we could to help us understand how finances worked. (There wasn't much.) Through those efforts and continued education, we developed a set of financial principles that have guided us through our married life.

Here are some of the money principles that have served us well over the years:

- ▶ Set both short- and long-term goals with clear measures.
- ▶ Stay focused. Keep "the main thing" "the main thing."
- ▶ Develop and work within a realistic budget/spending plan.
- ▶ Communicate clearly, openly, honestly, and regularly.
- ▶ Work hard.
- ▶ Find ways to maximize your income.
- ▶ Live beneath your means.
- ▶ Always save a portion of your income.
- ▶ Assume there will be a tomorrow, and prepare for it.
- ▶ If you want to make a major discretionary purchase, "Wait for it; work for it; and pay for it." (Jim Davis)
- ▶ Agree that both parties must approve expenditures above a certain level. Doing so gives each person veto power; so, use it carefully.
- ▶ Sweat the small stuff and the big stuff.
- ▶ Assume responsibility; take the initiative; and be proactive.
- ▶ Study and learn.

Going Broke is No Joke! is written in plain English and is easy to follow. Its main purpose is to help you understand basic money matters that will equip you with the knowledge you need to develop your own philosophy about money and make good financial decisions so you don't end up "going broke."

Over seven chapters, the book addresses a diverse collection of important money management topics often asked about or misunderstood. The first chapter challenges and guides you to understand your own financial values which may be the same as or different from those of the influential adults in your life. Subsequent chapters focus-in on a single, important money management topic such as spending plans, job loss, banking, credit, student loans, and money scams.

After a brief chapter introduction which sets the scene for that topic, the book lists several frequently-asked questions on the subject. Each question is then succeeded by a brief Money Tip, immediately followed by a more in-depth explanation based on my understanding of the environment relative to that particular issue. The seven chapters and 52 Money Tips address topics I think matter a lot to my audience and are those I am often asked about.

Usually, there is not a simple, pointed answer. Instead, the issue may be complex and intertwined with several other matters. I try to make the response as succinct as possible and often provide references if you want a more in-depth explanation. You may choose to read the book from cover-to-cover, or skip around in order of your interest.

This book is the culmination of more than 30 years I've spent educating myself; conducting seminars from coast to coast; advising individuals and couples, both rich and poor; and listening to people talk about their hopes, fears, misconceptions, mistakes, and misunderstandings about money. I'm writing about things I've studied, things I know and care about, and things I personally practice. (I suggest you consult legal and financial advisors before implementing any of my recommendations or suggestions to determine whether they are right for you.)

I hope you find *Going Broke is No Joke!* enlightening and easy to read and understand. My goal is to inspire you to take the financial actions necessary for you to lead the life you want.

Remember, your financial freedom is up to you. Today's decisions are the building blocks of tomorrow's realities!

Preface

Going broke is no fun, and it's definitely no joke!

The *American Heritage Dictionary* defines the term "**broke**" as "lacking funds or being bankrupt." Both can occur when you don't have enough income to cover your everyday expenses, or you have enough income to cover them, but your level of debt eats up any excess funds.

Many Americans find themselves in one or the other situation. The *Washington Post* recently reported that 46% of Americans above the poverty line said they could not come up with $400 to cover an emergency without borrowing the money from someone or using a credit card. According to the U.S. Census Bureau, the most recent census puts the U.S. population at 313 million with 266 million living above the poverty line. That means almost 122 million Americans (46% of 266) would not have the cash to cover the referenced $400 expense.

Research has shown that most people could avoid or escape these situations and improve their financial condition by learning and applying basic money management rules. Unfortunately, these rules are not taught in most schools, and often parents either do not know financial concepts or do not explain them to their children.

Today's money environment is complex and dynamic. In the past, many elements of our economy remained essentially unchanged for years at a time. Bank practices, credit procedures, interest rates, mortgage programs, and other financial elements operated consistently, changing very little over time. But, now, the financial landscape is in a constant state of flux. Here's how:

- ▸ New financial products are introduced almost daily.
- ▸ There are thousands of different credit cards and credit-card products available to evaluate and from which to choose.
- ▸ Laws and regulations are frequently changed or updated.
- ▸ New resources, such as the internet, now play a central role in many aspects of our financial lives.
- ▸ Online banking, electronic tax filing, and internet shopping are just the tip of the internet iceberg.
- ▸ The internet makes huge amounts of information available to manage our financial lives, but it also makes collection and availability of your personal data available to others. This online aggregation of data makes it relatively easy for scam artists to develop new schemes to trick you out of your hard-earned money. (Who hasn't received the email from the Nigerian prince asking you to help him get millions of dollars out of his country, a portion of which he will share with you, if only you will give him access to your checking account?)

A big problem in the money game is there has been no organized way to learn the rules. Neither the currency you get from an ATM nor the paycheck deposited in your bank account comes with a user's manual or operating instructions. So, how does one keep up with all of this and learn to effectively manage one's money, daily?

- ▸ One information source could be our parents, who taught us so many other things about life as we grew up. Indeed, some of us were fortunate enough to have a parent like Mimi or another adult in our lives who taught us the basic money management ropes. However, many others were not so fortunate, including those who saw their parents struggle with financial issues and demonstrate many of the wrong steps to manage their funds.

▶   A second obvious place one might expect to learn such important concepts is in our schools, where we are taught so many other life skills. Unfortunately, problems exist there, too. Until just a few years ago, very few states included financial literacy training as part of their curricula.

Even today, only 17 states mandate a course in financial literacy as a component of their core high school curriculum. (The National Financial Educators Council defines financial literacy as, "possessing the skills and knowledge on financial matters to confidently take effective action that best fulfills an individual's personal, family, and global community goals.")

Similarly, at the college level, money management courses are only now being introduced at selected colleges. As a result, millions of young people enter the economy and achieve the age when they can negotiate contracts, but do so with limited financial knowledge.

So, what does it take to win at the money game? As Mimi used to say, "Get something in your head so you can have something in your pocket." In other words, learn the rules of the money game and apply them vigorously in your day-to-day life, and you likely will be successful.

Many people find themselves in the workforce with significant living expenses; several credit cards with growing balances; little or no savings for emergencies, children's college expenses, or retirement; and no real roadmap for getting on a financially secure path. What do we do about this? These are some of the issues this book addresses.

Going Broke is No Joke! begins with the recognition that being "broke" can be challenging, embarrassing, stressful, and may even make you sick. I wrote this book to give you the knowledge you need to take control of your financial life. My intent is to share with you some of the key lessons I have learned after more than 40 years in the financial field.

I began that career working in the finance and accounting operations of several of America's major Fortune 500 corporations, culminating in my appointment as senior vice president of a major bank. In those positions, I created multi-million-dollar budgets, managed vast investment portfolios, oversaw payroll and accounting functions, and ran the back-office operations of a large regional bank.

For this book, I bring the knowledge and techniques gained in the corporate world; add an M.B.A. in finance and a Master of Science degree in personal financial planning; and call on my over 20 years of experience as a personal finance educator and counselor to provide answers to some of the questions you may have about financial rules and outcomes.

The good news is that the rules of effective money management can be learned, and, when applied, will help you improve your financial situation and begin saving for the future. The bad news is that if you refuse to apply these rules and carefully manage your financial life, you probably will end up broke.

As someone who has lived by these principles all of my life—and has taught and counseled thousands of people as a corporate and personal finance professional—I can assure you, if you decide to take control of your financial life and practice the money rules discussed in this book, you will see a substantial improvement in your finances and will reduce your stress over money.

CHAPTER 1

Plan to Avoid Being Broke
Know Yourself and Develop Your Strategy

Your own attitude about money along with your thirst for understanding the rules of the money game and the discipline required to win at playing it, all combine to determine the level of financial success you will likely have. Although, in our early years, we are conditioned by the adults in our lives, as we become adults ourselves, only we can make changes to those scripts and chart our own course.

Whether you end up going broke or having a lot of money is, in large part, determined by the money choices you make as an adult. Even if you become a member of a couple, each of you must determine your individual money attitudes and then that of the two of you as a unit. Hopefully, you discover you both are on the same page and have similar money goals and beliefs.

Perhaps, some of the questions below are familiar because they are the same as those you have thought about. If so, then the discussion following each one should help provide clarity regarding how you think about money and will guide you as you develop your own money strategies.

My parents were very tight-fisted with money when I was a child. Am I destined to have the same money attitude they had?

MONEY TIP #1: Not necessarily. You have the right to decide how you will handle your finances. Determine your own financial attitude about money, and then let that be your guiding principle throughout your life as you confront money matters.

Let me answer that question more fully. Resolve how you think about money—what having money means to you, what you want money to do for you, what your long-term life goals are, and how you feel about the possibility of being broke. Only then will you be able to develop a system that gets both your financial goals and personal values in sync. This may mean reverting to your parents' more conservative roots. It is just as likely to mean developing a whole new way of thinking that works for you—an adult who wants to take full control of and responsibility for your own financial future.

The habits of many of the adults in our lives—mother, father, grandparents, spouses, ex-spouses, etc.,—along with our childhood experiences involving money, affect each of us, seriously impacting how we think about money. They form the basis of our family values. Sometimes, we become like the adults who influenced us. Just as often, we become the exact opposite.

So, understanding your financial value system is essential to charting your own course and managing your financial life. This understanding is based on your own life experiences surrounding money. Some of these concepts you may want to adopt as part of your own money philosophy; others, you may not. The decision is yours to make to decide what money strategy you want to make your own.

In my own case, I had the example of a strong, knowledgeable woman who knew and understood the money rules, despite not having a lot of it. I wanted to be a lot like her and use knowledge and wit to ensure, to the extent possible, that I won at playing the money game.

By giving us an allowance (and refusing to give us more when we ran out), Mimi taught us how to budget. We didn't know that term while growing up, but we certainly came to know it after we became adults. In my view, a budget (or spending plan) is the money manager's "best friend."

Fortunately, I married a guy who has the same attitudes about money that I have. To this day, we use a budget to direct our spending and to help us stay on track toward meeting our individual and family goals. We are regular savers and never overspend because we both are always aware of our financial situation. You see, neither of us wants to end up broke.

When I think about Mimi's directive that we each had to learn to stand on our own two feet (to "paddle our own canoe"), I am reminded of another incident with her that has made me smile for years. Jim and I were visiting from out of town and were in her bedroom one afternoon, dressing to go out. Mimi knocked on the door and asked to come in to put money in her piggy bank. I asked where she had gotten money, since she had not been out of the house. She replied that her neighbor, Oscar, had given it to her. I asked why he had given her money. She said, "Because he used my phone." "You charge your neighbor to use your phone?" I asked, not believing what I had heard. "Yes, I do," she said, unapologetically.

"Why?" I inquired. She told me it was because there were three grown men in that house and they were too cheap to buy a phone.

When she told me, how much she charged them, I remarked that the amount was more than they would pay in a public phone booth. It was her witty reply to my last comment that still makes me smile. She said, "I charge them more for several reasons: one, my house is warm in the winter and cool in the summer; two, I give them a comfortable place to sit down; three, I save them a two-block walk to the phone booth; four, they don't have to have exact change; and five, they don't have to use my phone if they don't want to! Now, can I get to my bank, please?"

As you can see, she was an absolute believer in constantly teaching money values, regardless of one's age. They were passed on to us, and we have adopted many of her teachings as our own. (We may not be quite as rigid as she was, but we all believe in taking responsibility for one's own financial well-being.)

When does one need a financial advisor?

MONEY TIP #2: As you accumulate assets and/or feel the need for professional guidance to help chart your course, you will likely find the services of a financial advisor useful to help set your financial goals and plan.

There are at least three times you may need a financial advisor.
1.   To create a financial plan
2.   To manage your cash and investments
3.   To get a second (professional) opinion on how you're handling your money

Carefully choosing a financial advisor will keep you from making certain kinds of mistakes, including focusing on your

finances too late. There is no downside to getting help from a pro-
fessionally trained financial advisor.

I am an avid saver. Can I co-exist happily with a fiancé who is a carefree spender?

MONEY TIP #3: Yes, but, make sure you discuss your own financial and life goals, as well as his, with your prospective life partner BEFORE the wedding takes place.

When I do singles' seminars, I always recommend that participants exchange credit scores before exchanging wedding vows.
For those who may not be familiar with the term, your credit
score is a numerical representation of your default risk on loan
repayments, with a low number representing a higher risk for the
lender. Credit score values are derived from your credit history,
and range from 300 to 850. Low credit scores can result in higher
interest rates; an inability to have certain services put in your own
name, like utilities; lack of consideration for certain jobs; and an
inability to obtain credit in your own name.

The original credit (FICO) score was developed by Fair Isaac
Corp. It helps lenders and others predict how likely you are to make
your credit payments on time. The greater your credit score, the
higher the credit limit likely will be that the lender will grant you.

There are three major credit bureaus that maintain credit information and to which creditors regularly report your payment and
spending habits. They are Equifax, Experian, and TransUnion. (See
Appendix C for contact information for the three credit bureaus.)

You have three credit scores, one from each of the three credit
bureaus. Though they may be slightly different because not all

lenders report to each one, they tend to be in the same ballpark. The law says that once a year, any person can get one free credit report from each of the three bureaus. To do so, contact the credit bureau of choice or go online to www.annualcreditreport.com. Be forewarned, the report is free, but you will have to pay to get the actual score.

Let's get back to the original question. My suggestion that you exchange FICO scores may sound strange, but you need to know the spending habits of anyone with whom you are about to partner. It's one thing to have $100,000 in student loans. It's quite another to owe that same amount to Sears, Macy's, MasterCard, and Walmart. And, if there ever has been something as serious as a bankruptcy, the other person certainly has a right to know before the wedding. (There's a lot to be done between the time you say, "I will" and the time you say, "I do!")

A credit score exchange serves as the basis for financial discussions that, hopefully, will force the two of you to talk about attitudes about your own money; how you've handled money in the past (and why); and how the two of you want your financial future together to work, especially your desire to never end up broke. Once you start having these kinds of open and honest discussions, you will develop an understanding of and appreciation for each other's point of view. This should pave the way for compromises you both can find acceptable.

In one case I know of, it was not until the couple went to close on their first home that the new wife discovered her spouse's earlier bankruptcy, that he had been married before, and that he was under a court's child-support order. All of these things had a serious impact on his credit record and now, very likely, on hers. Imagine the arguments that occurred that evening and beyond! (I suspect the problem here was much greater than just a few financial omissions.)

In his book, *Smart Couples Finish Rich*, author David Bach says, "According to the experts, the number one cause of divorce in this country is fighting over money." Working together on your financial goals not only increases the likelihood that the two of you will succeed financially, but it also improves your chances of living "happily ever after."

So, the answer is, yes, you two can co-exist happily, if you do your homework and are open and honest with each other about your money views. But, don't kid yourself. Making this work might take several conversations; it might involve some pain; and neither of you is likely to get everything you want.

My significant other and I are about to move in together. I think we should have a written financial agreement; he doesn't. Who's right?

MONEY TIP #4: You are. You should protect your own financial future by writing a contract that makes clear any financial arrangements you enter into with a non-spouse.

Your question seems to center around whether there are protections each of you needs as you enter into this living arrangement. Indeed, there are.

Let's assume that you and your friend will buy property together; perhaps, have joint bank accounts; obtain credit; and accumulate other things of value. You need to have written agreements detailing who owes and who owns what and how things will be divided if the relationship does not work out. Unlike married couples, you may not have any automatic legal protections. Therefore, without written agreements as described above, you might not have the protection you need.

Imagine, for a moment, that you pooled your resources to buy a home, but your friend is the only one listed on the title.

What do you suppose will happen to the house if you decide to go your separate ways? Legally, the house belongs to the one whose name is on the title, and the other has no recourse. Even if you can prove that you helped make the monthly payments, the property still belongs to the titleholder, and you have no legal claim to any of the equity in the house. This is the reason you both need to make certain that "what if" possibilities are thought through, in advance, and written agreements are prepared and signed. That way, neither of you will end up feeling taken advantage of nor is either of you likely to lose your total "investment" in the property.

My fiancé thinks we should have joint credit cards but I'd rather not do that. He says there is no risk in merging our credit, since we intend to marry one day. Is there?

MONEY TIP #5: Yes, there is a significant risk, especially if the wedding doesn't take place. To guard against unexpected occurrences, keep your finances separate until after the wedding, and even then, only after you feel comfortable merging the two.

Many people think the way your fiancé does. But, you both should be aware that this poses several risks. First, the relationship may not work out and you may have to untangle a mess. Second, if you get joint cards, legally, you each will be responsible for the entire debt, regardless of who actually made the purchases. Third, your spending habits may be very different, and one could end up going broke paying for the other's excessive spending habits. You each should establish your own credit history in your own name. After your wedding is soon enough to open joint accounts.

My mother always kept a separate account my father didn't know about for "just in case." I am about to be married, and she advises me to do the same. Should I?

MONEY TIP #6: I don't believe in "secret" accounts. Instead, I suggest you have an open discussion with your fiancé about each of you having separate money for which only you are accountable. Do not engage in "financial infidelity!"

How you will manage your finances once you get married is something you and your fiancé should talk seriously about BEFORE you say, "I do." There are many ways couples may agree to handle their finances, as long as you are both in agreement.

Your mother's well-meaning message is intended to ensure that you have the resources needed to take care of yourself rather than have to be dependent upon your spouse. Some women have been known to keep cash "socked away" in a pair of old socks; in the back of a dresser drawer; or in an old purse. If you take her advice, she feels, you'll have a "stash of cash" you can pull from, if necessary.

I do not, personally, advocate secret accounts for either of you. You may each have a separate account that is yours alone to use and manage, but, why does it have to be a secret? (See Money Tip #8 below for a discussion of "financial infidelity.")

One compromise may be that each of you has an account of your own, funded regularly with an amount you both have agreed upon. Then, how you spend it is entirely up to you.

My spouse is a serious penny pincher. He drives around looking for the cheapest gas, dilutes liquid detergents, refuses to throw out dated foods and consumes them anyway, etc. It's driving me crazy, but, he says that's the way he was brought up and he's saving money. Is there anything I can do?

MONEY TIP #7: Perhaps there is. It's a lot of work, but try to find a counter to as many of his extreme penny-pinching ways as you can. Maybe, you will be able to eventually get him to see things your way, especially if you can prove his way is actually costing the family more than it saves.

This is a true case of living what one has learned. Your spouse grew up in a household where this was the norm, and he feels very comfortable continuing those practices. He actually is uncomfortable when he is not doing them.

Perhaps you can show him that some of the savings are not really savings at all. Driving around to find the cheapest gas actually wastes money on the excess driving. Diluting liquid detergents probably causes you to use twice as much of the thinner liquid, thereby negating the savings. Eating "old" food can lead to a medical problem, which may end up costing more than the value of the food you would toss out.

Being frugal can be beneficial. I have included more than two dozen money-saving tips in Money Tips #15 and #39.

My spouse has suddenly started acting very secretive about money. Could she be hiding either money or expenses, and is this what is meant by "financial infidelity?"

MONEY TIP #8: Yes, this could be a sign of "financial infidelity." If you suspect there is a serious issue, in a non-threatening way, have an open and honest discussion with your spouse about your money concerns and encourage her to do the same. Also, maintain an awareness of your financial situation.

"Financial infidelity" occurs when one spouse or relationship partner hides assets or debts, or commits other acts in secret that are detrimental to the couple's joint finances. It is not uncommon. One in three adults who said they'd co-mingled their finances also said they'd either committed or experienced an act of financial deceit, according to a January 2014 survey by the National Endowment for Financial Education, or NEFE, a Denver-based nonprofit.

If your partner has bank statements, credit card bills or other important financial information sent to his or her office instead of your home, deception could be at work. If you suspect your significant other has been financially unfaithful, here are some additional signs to look for:

- ▸ You're cut off from a joint credit card.
- ▸ You see no activity by your partner on a card you've normally both used.
- ▸ You receive statements in the mail from a financial institution you've never heard of.
- ▸ Your partner has lots of new possessions and experiences.

- ▸ Cash goes missing or is unaccounted for.
- ▸ Your partner is paranoid about getting the mail.
- ▸ Your partner becomes overly financially generous toward you, and you don't know how or why.

Rather than go on the attack, discuss the problem honestly and openly, and try to work together on a solution. If you cannot come to a resolution by yourselves, then seek counseling.

Several years ago, early one Saturday morning, a friend/neighbor showed up at our house, distraught. Her husband had just announced he was leaving the marriage. After her shock wore off, they spent time talking about who would get what asset. Things were going ok until she asked about their savings. He informed her they had spent all of their money. This caused problems for a couple of reasons. First, she knew that wasn't so. (They were both professionals and they lived way below their means.) Second, she had no idea of even the name of the financial institution where their money was kept because, by agreement, he handled all the family finances. She was devastated.

After he left, different than before, she had to open the mail and pay the bills. When she saw a charge on their credit card for the local Hilton, she got the confirmation she sought. This was a clear case of both financial and physical infidelity.

I think it's time to start teaching my children, who are 7 and 9, about money. My husband thinks they are too young. Are they?

MONEY TIP #9: No, they are not. Your children are old enough to understand the concept of money, so, it is time to start teaching them money rules.

I don't think it's ever too early to begin teaching children about money. When we were all very young, Mimi insisted my siblings and I learn how money works and develop a healthy respect for money. The allowance system she used formed the basics of money management for all of us. We had to learn to budget our money. It didn't matter how much (or how little) the allowance was. Basically, we had to make what we were given last for two weeks, until the next allowance day, or do without.

Teaching kids about money involves more than just counting coins. It involves teaching them about saving, spending, giving, investing and respecting money. Developing discipline is a very important part of this teaching.

I am licensed to teach a financial literacy program called "Camp Millionaire." It is a one- to five-day program, filled with fun and games, and teaches kids, teens and adults about money. In that program, using age-appropriate language, we teach such things as:

- ▸ The many roles of money
- ▸ The rules of the game of money
- ▸ How to live within your means (allowances and budgets)
- ▸ How to use your money to create the life you want
- ▸ Money beliefs—what some of them are and where they come from
- ▸ Types of income—earned versus passive
- ▸ The three pillars of wealth—real estate, business, and the stock market
- ▸ Needs versus wants
- ▸ Using other people's money, i.e., credit
- ▸ Making dream boards, i.e., imagining what you want your tomorrow to look like

To date, under the Creative Wealth International banner, Camp Millionaire's instructors have taught thousands of people—ages 8 to 80—the rules of the money game. The organization is committed to providing financial education to people worldwide, but, children, teens and women are a major program focus. (You can go online to www.creativewealthintl.org to learn about program offerings in your area and other financial education products offered.)

Another valuable resource for financial literacy tools for young people is the website for an organization called NEFE—the National Endowment for Financial Education—at www.nefe.org. NEFE is a "...private, non-profit, national foundation wholly dedicated to improving the financial well-being of all Americans" and provides lots of useful, free information.

The type of instruction Camp Millionaire, NEFE and others offer, helps give people of all ages a basis for developing the solid money sense that is critical to have going forward and keeping them from running out of money. However, where kids are concerned, the best thing you can do is lead by example. Early on, make discussions about money a family affair and give your youngsters head starts on their journeys toward financial freedom. As they get older and can absorb more, teach them more. Each of you will be glad you did.

Should a child's allowance be connected to chores? In my circle of friends, most of whom have young teens, some say "yes;" others say "no!"

MONEY TIP #10: No. I believe the two should be kept separate. Use the allowance primarily to teach basic money management skills. Chores should be used to emphasize work and the work ethic.

According to Dr. Deborah Gilboa, a family physician in Pittsburgh who focuses on parenting and youth development, "Chores are really important, but they should be used to teach kids how to help out." She went on to say, "If you connect chores and money, then, it's a job and the child can quit. The child has to learn that he/she must do chores because they are a member of the household and that's what we do."

Dr. Gilboa suggests that parents use chores as a lesson about work ethic, and allowance as a way to teach kids about money. Since they will have money of their own someday, it's a perfect time to start educating them about saving, spending, budgeting, donations, etc.

One might say I'm biased, having grown up in a household where allowance was the name of the game. This money was not given in payment for doing chores or anything else for that matter. Chores were done because that's what we were told was our responsibility to the household.

On the other hand, allowances were given both to teach us financial responsibility, and so we could have a small amount of money of our own. Having an allowance taught us how to budget our money, and how to choose between needs and wants.

I have a decent job and not many expenses. Shouldn't I be able to spend $5 to $10 a day on lunch if I want to?

MONEY TIP #11: Yes, you should. But, that isn't the point. Try cutting back on the daily lunch expenditure and put the amount saved in a separate account where you can see the impact as your savings grow.

Buying lunch every day is costly, especially given the alternative of bringing lunch from home most days and then splurging, say, once a week. Let's do the math. Assume there are 46 work weeks in the year after allowing for 6 weeks of vacation, sick days, and holidays. This comes out to a total of 230 workdays (46 weeks x 5 days). At your average cost of $7.50 (halfway between $5 and $10), you spend slightly more than $1,700 a year on daily lunch purchases. If you were to carry your lunch from home regularly and save even $1,000 of this amount, your bank account would be richer by a nice tidy sum.

Why should I save part of my income when I have so little money left after I pay my bills?

MONEY TIP #12: You should save because having savings is a way of taking care of yourself and of providing protection against unforeseeable financial emergencies.

Many people find it challenging to save a portion of their income. They say that due to the high level of their current expenses, they cannot include a savings line in their budget. At the same time, they understand that having little or no excess funds in the bank presents its own set of problems.

There are at least four strong reasons why everyone, regardless of their financial situation, should either begin saving a portion of their income immediately, or set a date certain when they will start a serious savings campaign, and then create a spending plan that gets them to that goal. The four major reasons to begin a long-term savings program are:

▸ **Unexpected expenses.** No matter how well you plan your expenses, there is always the possibility that either you overlooked something, or, more likely, something completely unforeseeable occurs (e.g., a major car repair, an unexpected tax bill, braces for your child, or unexpected medical bills), and you do not have the funds to cover that expense. For emergencies, many financial experts recommend that you have enough savings to cover six to eight months of living expenses.

▸ **Planned expenses.** Let's face it, we all want to have nice things or do fun things in our lives and, most often, those things cost money. A birthday party, a vacation trip, or even dinner out at a nice restaurant are fun treats to break the monotony of daily life. Having savings in the bank for just such situations means you don't have to do without or go into debt to finance those activities.

▸ **College expenses.** Research has shown that fewer and fewer new jobs can be filled by people with high school diplomas. In the coming years, your children will need to have at least some education beyond high school, if not a college degree, to be competitive in the job market. Parents should be prepared to pay at least a portion of those expenses to spare their children the burden of high levels of student loan debt, which could limit their future options.

▸ **Retirement.** After working 30, 40 or 50 years, most of us look forward to a long retirement doing the fun things we like, but may not have had time to do during our working life. Funding those activities (fishing, golfing, traveling, etc.) while covering everyday bills during retirement is a challenge we all must face. Social Security is generally not sufficient to cover 100% of retirement expenses, and pension retirement sources may not be sufficient either. So, putting away money in the form of a 401K, IRA, or other regular savings is the only remaining option.

In addition to the above, saving money is a good way to take care of yourself, is good financial discipline, and is the best way to get ahead. You can start saving a small amount that increases as you get salary increases, gifts, tax refunds, etc. You'd be amazed at how quickly even small savings add up.

Did you realize if you save the cost of a soft drink or bottled water (@$1 per day, minimum), at the end of the first year, you would have saved over $350? At the end of 10 years, you would have saved over $3,500, excluding inrerest.

CHAPTER 2

Why You Need a Spending Plan

Make Sure Your In-come Does Not Exceed Your Out-go

Of all the financial topics I teach, the idea of creating and living by a budget or spending plan is the one that gets the most negative reactions. All kinds of reasons are given for not having one.

- ▸ I don't know how to make one.
- ▸ Making a budget is hard.
- ▸ I can't stick to a budget, so, why make it?
- ▸ A budget is too restrictive. If I try to live by one, I can't do any of the things I want to do.

I contend that taking the time to review your past expenses and to plan for those you expect (or want) to have over the next 6-12 months, in the end, gives you more freedom, not less. Yes, it takes time to do it properly. But, when you have created it, you will have an excellent picture of what you can and cannot afford to do over the time period the plan covers.

To the extent you have included **ALL** of your expected income and expenses, provided for savings, and have created an emergency fund, your financial life is much more simplified. After you run the numbers (subtracting expenses from income each month) and make the needed adjustments until the two are in balance, you know what you can and cannot do, if you stick to the plan. Each month, you aren't worrying about whether you can pay the rent, insurance, school expenses, etc. They are all in your budget; it balances; so, you can chill.

I may be different than most people, but, I find having a detailed, thoughtfully-crafted spending plan to be one of the most "free-ing" things I do. I never have to wonder whether an expense can be paid as long as my spouse and I stick to the plan.

A budget is not set in stone. As life happens, you then make the necessary adjustments to your plan to reflect those changes. I challenge you to follow the steps outlined in Appendix B and give it a try. I think you'll be glad you did.

Is it true that people who follow a budget or spending plan are more likely to meet their financial goals than those who do not?

MONEY TIP #13: My own experience, and that of many I have counseled is yes, they are. Think about your long-term goals. Then, set up an initial 12-month spending plan that reflects those goals and see whether following that plan provides a better roadmap for you than would have been the case without it. I think you will find that it does.

People who follow a budget not only are more likely to meet their financial goals, but also, they spend less, save more, pay with cash or pay off their credit cards at the end of each billing cycle, and are less likely to "go broke."

Planners are more likely to take a long-term view of their goals and are willing to make the needed sacrifices to achieve them. While most indeed work to make sure they have an emergency fund of six to eight months of living expenses, many also have begun to create funding mechanisms for events far into the future, like college funding for themselves or a loved one, retirement, and long-term care.

People who set up a budget or plan to manage their spending are comfortable setting priorities, making choices and, in general, are willing to accept responsibility for themselves and their families. They seem to understand and live by the old adage that says, "When your out-go exceeds your in-come, your up-keep will be your down-fall!"

Does having a spending plan have to be restrictive?

MONEY TIP #14: No, it does not. You should develop a spending plan that balances your resources and priorities. Then, review it regularly, and make adjustments as your life circumstances change.

If the spending plan is done properly, it does not have to limit you. Its purpose is not to restrict you financially, but rather to provide you with an enormous amount of flexibility to apply your resources as you see fit, but within the limits of those resources.

It is neither a straight-jacket nor a shackle. It is not an inflexible tool and is not a plan that must be followed forever, no matter what.

A spending plan is a step-by-step roadmap for meeting your expenses during a given period of time. If it is done honestly and completely, it covers, at a minimum, a 6-to-12-month timeframe and provides an at-a-glance summary of all of your income and expenses during that period. It shows where you may have the flexibility to alter your spending.

It also helps you account for money that just seems to trickle away. It provides a way for family members to talk about financial goals for the household and the role of each in achieving them. This effort has the added benefit of putting everyone in the household on the same page. Plus, it provides you with a roadmap for gaining control over your money. A spending plan is flexible and should be adjusted as your life changes.

Once all of your known and anticipated income/expenses for the selected period are listed, a spending plan can help reduce stress due to money worries. If you follow the roadmap you create, then your financial life can operate, essentially, on auto-pilot.

I tell my clients, "When you can do better, you do better, not the other way around." That means you don't spend first and hope your income is sufficient to cover your expenditures. With a proper spending plan, you are certain to match the two at the outset. (See Appendix B for a sample spending plan with instructions on how to make one.)

I admit to being a master budgeter. As a veteran finance professional, I have done hundreds of budgets in corporate America, for clients in my financial advisory practice, and for my family.

Allow me to use my household of two adults as an example. Usually, around November, my husband and I start discussing financial goals for the next year—places we want to go, things we want to do, and out-of-the-ordinary expenses we might incur. This conversation continues off and on over the next few weeks. By early December, our decisions have been converted into dollars, and I have done a draft of the next year's budget. Then, we let it rest until the new year's tax rates, other deductions, and the prior year-end expenses are known. By the end of January, the budget is set for the year, pending major life changes.

Because we have been doing this for a long time and know our spending patterns, few surprises come up during the year. There are times when we may decide to do something that is unplanned. But, because we are savers, spontaneous decisions always can be funded from savings. I can proudly say that we never, ever over-spend. If we don't have the money, we do without until we do.

I ran into a woman recently who had been one of my early clients. She's on a steady course now but still thinks about one of our budget sessions in which she asked how she was supposed to pay for her cigarettes given the skimpy amount allocated for her allowance. She remembers my response as though it was yester-day, "I hate to be the one to tell you, but you're too poor to smoke!" We all have to decide what's important and what we are willing to do without to achieve our goals.

I have tried and tried to find ways to save money, but can't seem to find any. I always "run out of money before I run out of month." I hate being broke all the time. What can I do?

MONEY TIP #15: Pay close attention to where you spend money and be on the lookout, constantly, for coupons and dis-counted products and services consistent with those you use.

As the title of the book says, going broke is no joke. When you have financial challenges, the first thing you have to do is be willing to face them. Then, you have to decide whether there are ways to increase your income. If not, expense reduction is the only other alternative.

There are many ways to save money. You just have to make up your mind that you are willing to make the changes needed to achieve your goal. Some adjustments will be more painful than others.

Here are 40 money-saving tips to jumpstart your thinking:

1. Buy a membership to a big-box discount store like Costco or Sam's Club. The items discounted range from food to health supplies, autos and auto parts, appliances, and travel. At an annual cost of about $50 per person, the savings will quickly cover the membership fee, especially if you make significant purchases. (Note: You often can buy pharmaceuticals at these stores, even if you are not a member.)

2. If you are an avid bottled water drinker, consider buying water in the 24-36 bottle pack in either the discount store or a big-box store and taking your own water to work or on outings. The same goes for snacks you like to munch on during the day. The savings of $2 to $5 per day easily adds up to more than $500 per year.

3. Spend less on food by shopping with a list and with coupons.

4. Ask your physician and pharmacist for generic drugs, whenever appropriate, as they are usually much less expensive than their brand name equivalents.

5. When taking a drug for a long time, consider using mail-order pharmacies which often charge lower prices for a 90-day supply.

6. Buy eyeglasses on line. There are many discount optical sites, like www.zennioptical.com.

7. Save hundreds of dollars annually by comparing prices at local gasoline stations and by using the lowest octane rating called for in your car's owner's manual.

8. Save on gas by keeping your engine tuned.

9. To determine the recommended mileage for an oil change for your vehicle, go to www.checkyournumber.org to find the correct number for your car. Changing the oil every 3,000 miles / 6 months is old school. Newer models use synthetic oils, and they last much longer.

10. Keep tires inflated to the manufacturer's recommended pressure so as not to reduce gas mileage by running on deflated tires.

11. Enroll in gas rewards programs at local grocery stores. You may even share the program with friends and family so points add up faster. (These programs can save you as much as 20 cents per gallon on gas.)

12. If you have a carrier on top of your car, remove it, if possible, when it's not being used. According to AAA, carriers can reduce gas mileage by as much as 25%.

13. If your teenaged driver gets good grades, see if your insurance company offers a "good student discount."

14. If you are a senior citizen, take a driving class. Many insurers offer up to a 15 percent discount for older drivers who take an online safety course.

15. If your car is driven under 5,000 miles annually, ask your insurance company for a low-mileage discount.

16. Save hundreds of dollars in finance charges by shopping for the cheapest auto loan, if you are in the market.

17. Vow to pay your credit cards off each month to save on interest payments. (In other words, buy no more than you can afford to pay for when the bill comes in.)

18. If you are unable to pay off a large credit card balance, pay as much as you can, and switch to a credit card that has

a low annual interest rate and does not assess a fee for a balance transfer.

19. When looking for a credit card, consider one that offers "cash back" since, often, you can convert your earned credits to dollars and use them to make monthly payments.

20. Consider refinancing your mortgage if you can get a rate that is at least one percentage point lower than your existing mortgage interest rate, and you plan to keep your new mortgage for at least three to five years. Be very careful about refinancing costs, and make sure they are not so high as to negate the value of the refinancing savings.

21. Enroll in online banking and online credit card features that categorize your purchases/spending. At the end of the statement cycle and at year end, review your categorized purchases to see how much money has been spent where. These online services can serve as a guide when making your new spending plan, and allow you to set budget thresholds and send alerts if your spending threatens pre-set levels.

22. To save as much as hundreds of dollars a year on electricity, make certain any new appliances you buy, especially air conditioners, refrigerators and furnaces, are "energy efficient."

23. Enroll in load-management programs and off-hour rate programs offered by your local electric utility. This may save you hundreds of dollars each year in electricity costs.

24. If you use a wireless phone, be sure the services you are paying for meet your needs and do not exceed your typical call and data usage patterns.

25. Unplug your cellphone and other electronics as soon as

they are fully charged so you're not wasting energy they continue to soak it up overnight.

26. When you boil water, boil only as much as you need. Otherwise, you're wasting energy to heat the extra amount.

27. Install a programmable thermostat.

28. Change all of your showerheads to water-saving models, and, if possible, buy low-flow toilets.

29. Contact a local dental school to get information about free or low-cost care.

30. Get a beauty school hairdo or haircut; or learn to do your hair and nails yourself rather than going to a salon.

31. Ask if a merchant offers a discount to people with disabilities and/or their escorts. Many do, but don't advertise it. Discounts may apply in areas like recreation, utilities, communications devices, travel and home modifications. www.DisabledDiscounts.com is one of the online resources for finding discounts for the disabled.

32. Contact your county to see whether it offers free income tax preparation for people with incomes below a certain level.

33. Shop at dollar stores for cheap items like toiletries, greeting cards, and some household goods, if you like getting a bargain.

34. Again, if you like bargain shopping, locate yard sales at www.yardsaletreasuremap.com which displays Craigslist local postings in your area and gives you a suggested driving route on a Google map.

35. Unless you're traveling with a lot of people or a lot of luggage, if you must rent a car, reserve a cheaper, compact car with better fuel efficiency. Compacts are popular and, if the company runs out of them, you might get a free upgrade.

36. After a certain time, kids eat free or for a discount at many chain restaurants. Check out the website www.familyfriendlyamerica.com for information on local eateries with this policy.

37. Before eating out, look for coupons for your destination at www.Restaurant.com. Upon request, many chain eateries offer a senior discount. Denny's, AppleBees, Boston Market, Chic-Fil-A, select IHOPs, and Wendy's just are a few of the big chain restaurants that discount senior meals or have senior menus.

38. Celebrate birthdays with a free meal. The website www.people.com/food/birthday-free-food-restaurants/ has a list of 88 major eateries that offer free items on your special occasion.

39. Skip extended warranties on purchases. Most major credit cards offer extended-warranty coverage for free.

40. If you are a senior, check with local colleges to see whether they offer free auditing for seniors. Some colleges permit seniors to attend any class for free.

Is making a spending plan easy? Can't you merely guess what your income and expenses will be during the time period it covers?

MONEY TIP #16: No, it is not easy. To put one together, gather all of the information mentioned below and find yourself a quiet place to take a first cut at a spending plan for yourself and your family. Then, take the time to review it with affected family members to make sure all priorities have been addressed.

Make no mistake, putting together a spending plan takes thinking and planning. It is not a guessing game. To do it properly, you need to gather a lot of information about past expenses and spending habits, estimate income and expenses for the future, and develop goals for the period covered. (See Appendix B for a sample.)

Look back at 6 to 12 months of expenses to determine both the categories and amounts of income and expenses to be reflected in your plan. To make sure you have as accurate information as possible, use sources like:

- ▸ Check registers
- ▸ Bank and credit card statements
- ▸ Bill stubs such as utilities, rent, mortgage insurance, child care, repairs, property taxes, gasoline, personal items, gifts, insurance, medical expenses, and transportation (including car payments, if any, repair/maintenance charges, tags, etc.)
- ▸ Tax returns
- ▸ Pay stubs
- ▸ Your written goals for the next 6 to 12 months and the costs associated with each

Use all of these pieces of information to put together the first draft of a plan that realistically reflects your (and your family's) income and expenditure patterns. Remember the saying, "GIGO" which means "Garbage In, Garbage Out." The plan won't be helpful to you if it isn't realistic. Then, make the adjustments needed to bring it into balance.

While it may take an extended period of time to set up your spending plan, it will pay off dramatically in helping you save more money by keeping your expenses under control.

CHAPTER 3

Bank on It

Discover Your Options and Choose Wisely

According to the FDIC (Federal Deposit Insurance Corporation), there were almost 6,800 commercial banks in the U.S. as of early 2014. At year end 2015, there were close to 6,200 credit unions.

Almost every adult in the U.S. deals with a financial institution on a regular basis. Together, these institutions provide a menu of services most of us find helpful in the conduct of our daily lives. Some of the services they provide include:

- ▶ Checking accounts
- ▶ Savings accounts
- ▶ Debit/credit cards
- ▶ Auto loans
- ▶ Mortgage loans
- ▶ Overdraft protection

Given this large array of services and the wide variety of institutions available both online and as brick-and-mortar buildings, it is imperative that we understand the services offered and the fees charged by our institutions of choice. The purpose of this chapter is to provide an aid to that understanding.

Bank fees are costing me a fortune. Can I do anything to lower them?

MONEY TIP #17: Yes, you can. Know the rules associated with each bank account you have and make a plan to use those accounts in a way that minimizes fees.

▸ You can avoid many bank fees, including those that are "hidden." First, you must understand them, and then, develop strategies to help you avoid them.

▸ Some of the "hidden" bank fees you can easily eliminate include:

- **Paper statement fees**—Charge for having your account statement mailed to you versus viewing it online. View your statement online, and, then, print a copy for your files.

- **Check imaging fees**—Charge for having copies of cancelled checks mailed to you with your monthly statement. View the cancelled check online, and, then, print it from your own printer, if/when you need a copy.

- **Overdraft transfer fees**—Charge for transferring money from another account in the same bank to your checking account to minimize/eliminate overdraft fees. Set up alerts for your checking account so you can be notified and transfer money into that account before an overdraft happens.

- **Excess activity fees**—Charge occurs when you exceed the federally-mandated limit on withdrawals and transfers for a particular type of account. Do transactions in person or through an ATM, as they are excluded from this limit.

- **ATM fees**—Most of these charges are due to out-of-network or excess activity fees. Though it takes discipline, to minimize ATM fees, write yourself a check or withdraw money from an ATM in your bank or credit union's network, once a week or so, to cover your budgeted/anticipated cash needs. That way, you will have the cash to pay for your expenses and will not need to constantly go back to the ATM. But, remember you have to make this amount last for the entire time period covered by the withdrawal.

  If taking out cash on a weekly basis doesn't work for you, there still are ways to minimize your ATM fees. Look on the back of your ATM card for the logo that indicates to which ATM network your bank belongs. While you may be charged by the in-network bank, at least **your** bank will not charge you an out-of-network fee. Also, you can check your bank's website for a listing of surcharge-free ATMs. In short, choose a local bank or credit union that belongs to a network that allows free use of ATMs in the network.

  There are surcharge-free networks like Star, Allpoint and Co-op Financial that claim to have thousands of ATMs nationwide. Another alternative is to use banks such as Metropolitan Bank (headquartered in Tennessee), and Schwab Bank (headquartered in California) that are not a part of any network but will reimburse you for ATM charges you incur.

There is another way to avoid ATM fees. Use only your bank's ATMs. Usually, there is no charge for their use unless you use them excessively or have an account that restricts your usage. One final thought—go inside the bank for the cash needed. This will eliminate ATM fees altogether.

In one case, a student who lives in one state and works in another, had her paycheck direct deposited into a bank in yet another state, thereby generating a large number of foreign ATM charges. When I asked why she uses an out-of-state bank, she replied that many years ago, her grandparents had started the bank where her paycheck was deposited, and she felt an emotional attachment to it. I suggested she maintain her relationship with that bank through a savings or other no-fee account, and find a local bank where her paycheck could be automatically deposited with more options for accessing her money without "foreign" ATM charges. With her current arrangement, she always had to incur charges to get her own funds. That was a huge waste of money.

There are several ways you can protect yourself from other bank fees:

▸ Understand your bank's check and deposit processing policies and practices—processing cutoff times; holiday processing schedule; holds on out-of-state checks, etc.

The bank should have available written material describing these policies and procedures.

▸ To eliminate non-sufficient funds (NSF) charges, don't write checks (or use your debit card), or use your bank's online bill pay feature unless you are certain you have the money in your account at the time of the transaction.

▸ Balance your checking account every month to ensure all of the transactions you have made have been recorded properly.

▸ Out-of-town or very large checks you deposit still might take several days to be credited to your account. So, again, be sure these deposits indeed are available to you before trying to withdraw those funds.

If your bank makes a mistake, the law says they must make the correction to your account within 10 business days of your notification and proof of the error, and that you must notify them of the error within 60 days. After 60 days, the bank's obligation is zero. For specific policies and instructions, you should read the "Terms and Conditions" found as a part of your electronic and/or paper statement in the area generally termed "In Case of Error."

Are debit cards always better to use than credit cards, since I don't have to pay interest on my purchases if I use them?

MONEY TIP #18: Not necessarily. There are advantages and disadvantages to using both. Take a look at the particular situation and decide which is better—debit or credit—given the pluses and minuses described below.

Debit cards are not always better to use than credit cards. There are benefits to both. Credit cards allow you to buy now and pay later (without interest charges, if you pay the bill in full each month before the due date). Each time you use a credit card, you are borrowing money from the bank that issued the card, and, then, repaying the loan. One of the major benefits of using credit cards for some purchases is that they offer very generous protections against fraudulent charges and disputes with merchants. Some have great rewards programs; some even offer free vacation cancellation/trip insurance. (Credit card laws and practices are discussed, in detail, in the next chapter on Credit.)

On the other hand, debit cards look like credit cards but operate very differently. Using a debit card is the same as paying cash. Funds are usually withdrawn from your bank account immediately, at the time of purchase, for the total amount of the purchase. There never are interest charges attached. With a debit card, you don't have to carry cash or checks, and the card provides instant access to your money, worldwide. However, there may be foreign transaction fees if you are out of the country when you use the card.

Below are a few debit card pitfalls:

▸ If you spend more than you have in your account, you may be allowed to make the purchase/withdrawal, but also you may incur substantial NSF fees. According to a recent Consumer's Union report, "...a person using a debit card more than 20 times per year pays an average of $223 in bounced check/overdraft fees. The one who doesn't use a debit card at all pays an average of $35."

▸ Debit card features—instant access to your money and, often, no required PIN (personal identification number)—make fraud much easier (and potentially costlier) than is the case with a credit card. Your bank account can be quickly drained if your debit card is lost or stolen and you do not report the loss to your bank immediately. However, the law limits your liability for unauthorized use of your debit card to $50 if reported within 2 days after you discover it missing. It increases that amount to $500 if you report it after 2 days but less than 60 days. Your loss becomes whatever has been taken out of your account if you fail to report an unauthorized transfer within 60 days after your bank statement containing the unauthorized use is mailed to you. However, your maximum loss under federal law for the unauthorized use of a credit card, if you report it stolen, is capped at $50.

▸ Unlike what routinely happens with the use of a credit card, if you have a problem with merchandise or a service purchased using a debit card, there is no "debit card company" available to help you resolve an issue with the vendor. For example, if the merchandise is defective, is not as represented, or you want to return it according to the return policy but the vendor won't allow you to, you may have to work that out by yourself.

▸ A credit card issuer often will withhold payment to a vendor until a dispute has been resolved. When you use a debit card to buy something, this option rarely exists; the bank usually does not temporarily refund your cash.

My bank automatically signed me up for overdraft protection and says I have no choice but to keep it. I think the charges are outrageous and I don't want that service! Are they correct?

MONEY TIP #19: No, they are not. You do have a choice. Current law says customers must opt in to have overdraft protection. However, to avoid overdraft fees, make sure you have funds in your account before you try to spend the money.

Overdraft protection is a service offered by most financial institutions that allows checking account holders to essentially spend money they don't have. The bank pays for the purchase or allows you to withdraw money from your account using a debit card or check, despite the absence of funds in your account, and then charges you a fee for doing so. That fee ranges from $15 to $39 per transaction, depending upon the institution. An **overdraft fee** is the bank's charge to you for letting the charge/withdrawal go through despite you not having enough money in your account to cover the expense.

The Federal Reserve passed a rule, effective July 1, 2010, that bans banks from charging overdraft fees unless customers sign up for the service. This decision was in response to many complaints from consumers about excessive overdraft fees they were being charged, often for very small overages, and, in many cases, even though they had not signed up for overdraft protection. By law, banks must send consumers a notice explaining their overdraft policies and fees. You, then, must be given the option of signing up for the service if you want it. It no longer can be automatic.

Overdraft fees are a multibillion-dollar revenue stream for financial institutions. According to *Forbes Magazine*, in 2015, banks and credit unions collected $32.5 billion in overdraft protection charges. Some consumers may welcome the service, even when it has not been requested. Others don't, especially if they find themselves paying hundreds of dollars in charges for a series of small transactions. (Overdraft fees average close to $35 per occurrence.)

Forbes also reported the following interesting statistics for 2015:

- ▶ 18% of Americans over-drafted their account within the previous year.
- ▶ 64% of people who over-drafted their account made less than $30,000 per year.
- ▶ The average checking account fees per account holder **without** overdraft protection was $28.
- ▶ The average checking account fees per account holder **with** overdraft protection was $119!

I once had a client who had $242 in bank fees on his checking account statement in one month. He was unaware his overdraft protection cost him $39 each time he activated it. Although he had no money in his account at the time, twice a month, he typically made a $20 withdrawal for each of the 3 days immediately preceding his bi-weekly payday, for a total of $117 in fees to withdraw $60! If he had withdrawn all $60 at once, at least he would have incurred only one $39 fee. He had no idea his actions were costing him that much money until I unsealed and reviewed several account statements with him. Of course, he could avoid the overdraft fees altogether if he didn't have the overdraft protection. (The bank just would not have allowed the withdrawals to go through.) What he really needed was to work with a financial advisor on learning the rules of the money game; set up a spending plan; and enforce some serious restrictions on himself to ensure he had both a longer-term view of his financial life and sufficient funds available when he needed them.

Is it true that it takes, on average, three days for a local check to clear? If so, doesn't that mean I can write a check without having the funds in my account for at least a couple of days after I write it?

MONEY TIP #20: Neither statement is true. Checks are clearing much faster today given new technology used by banks. So, you need to have the funds in your account when you write a check. Keep a watchful eye on your account balance to avoid bounced checks and overdraft fees, if you have overdraft protection.

It no longer takes local checks up to three days to clear. Under the Check Clearing for the 21st Century Act that went into effect in October 2004, checks could clear your bank within a few hours, instead of a few days. Thus, the time between when you write a check and when your bank processes it has been shortened considerably.

Under the 2004 law, banks can make digital copies of your checks and transmit the information through the checking system. They, then, can destroy the actual check. In some cases, a merchant merely digitizes your check and gives it right back to you before you leave the store.

However, you must be careful. Under this law, banks are not required to credit your account with deposits any more quickly than they did before the law. Thus, they are permitted to speed up withdrawals without speeding up the processing of deposits. Consumers Union estimates that this law results in millions of bounced checks and millions of dollars in associated bank fees because withdrawals are processed faster, but, deposits made to cover the checks still take the longer amount of time.

Also, many financial institutions now are posting to accounts throughout the day, not just at the end of the day. So, again, the extra time you had to cover a check when processing was done only once a day, is gone.

For some people, overdraft fees are a convenient way to guard against the embarrassment and costs associated with bounced checks. They don't mind the fees.

Bank policies vary and can change over time. Some banks don't charge overdraft fees if an account is overdrawn by $5 or less at the end of the business day. Many allow the charge to go through without a penalty. For example, if you buy a $10 lunch with just $6 in your account, you would be exempt from an overdraft fee and could enjoy your lunch because the charge would go through.

Outside of the banks without overdraft coverage fees, you may find a cheaper overdraft service at your bank called "overdraft protection transfers." These are opt-in programs that link a second account to your checking account. An overdraft would trigger a transfer from the second account to cover the transaction. The linked account can be a savings account, credit card, line of credit, or even another checking account, depending on the bank's policy. Though the cost of this transfer averages around $10, sometimes, it is less. So, shop around.

Overdraft fees, especially from overdraft protection, are some of the highest fees banks charge. Knowing how much these fees are might help you decide to opt out of the programs or find less expensive overdraft alternatives your bank may offer.

What is the difference between a credit union and a bank? Which is better?

MONEY TIP #21: There is no definitive answer to that question. If you are in the market for an account or a loan, compare the fees and services of both credit unions and banks, and then decide which is the better financial organization to service your needs.

Credit unions and banks offer many of the same services— checking accounts, savings accounts, personal loans, and more.

But, they have their differences, too. Credit unions are nonprofit, tend to have better product rates and fees, and usually offer localized, more personal customer service. Contrarily, banks are for-profit and some offer more innovative products. Neither is "better" than the other. Your own personal situation dictates which is more appropriate for you at a particular time.

Some of the areas of difference are described below.

ELIGIBILITY

- ▸ A bank is free to conduct business with any customer.
- ▸ By law, credit union membership is restricted to certain groups of affiliated people based on where they live, work, worship or attend school. Those who belong to a particular group, association or organization may also qualify. Sometimes, you can qualify if another member of your family or household is a member of the credit union.

PRODUCTS AND SERVICES

- ▸ Commercial banks, especially large ones, frequently offer many financial products and services beyond just consumer banking. In some cases, their size and financial clout allow them to offer a wider range of consumer products and services than credit unions.
- ▸ Credit unions tend to be more narrowly focused on financial services for consumers. While some may offer accounts for small businesses, credit unions concentrate more on their members' personal financial needs. Although the range of credit union financial products may be narrower than those offered by banks, they seek to make up for it by offering better interest rates, lower fees, and more personal service.

ACCESSIBILITY & CUSTOMER SERVICE

▶ Banks can be any size, but even the largest credit union does not match the branch and ATM networks of most medium-sized banks. Banks tend to provide greater access to services, like 24/7 customer service, weekend hours, and the latest advances in electronic and mobile banking.

To compensate for their limited presence, many credit unions have joined ATM- and branch-sharing networks to provide their members more convenient access to services. Nonetheless, a number of credit unions still offer limited hours, and some smaller credit unions don't provide electronic banking services, mobile banking apps or even ATM cards at all. But, what credit unions lack in physical presence, they tend to make up for with superior customer service. In 2014, banks scored 76 out of 100 points on the American Customer Satisfaction Index, compared with 85 points for credit unions.

FEES, INCENTIVES & RATES

▶ Banks routinely charge higher fees than credit unions. And, compared with credit unions, banks commonly offer their customers lower interest rates on deposit accounts and charge higher interest rates on loans.

▶ Credit unions' fees, such as overdraft fees, non-sufficient funds fees, and ATM fees, tend to be lower than banks. Membership requires a deposit of as little as $5, and most do not require a minimum daily balance to avoid fees. In general, credit unions offer higher rates of return on savings accounts, especially high-yield products such as money market accounts and certificates of deposit (CDs).

BUSINESS STRUCTURE

- ▸ Banks are for-profit financial companies and can be large or small, national, regional, or local. In most cases, they are public companies, which means they are led by a paid board of directors. As with other companies in the public domain, the ultimate owners are the bank's shareholders who purchase company stock as an investment for which they expect a financial return.

- ▸ Credit unions are not-for-profit financial cooperatives that are typically small and local. They are run by member-owners on a one member-one vote system. Under this structure, members agree on all of the cooperative's decisions together. Unlike a bank's paid board, directors at most credit unions are unpaid volunteers who are elected by a vote of the members. Credit union profits are regularly distributed to members in the form of dividends; a bank's profits are not.

CHAPTER 4

Understanding Credit
Know the Rules and Play by Them

by Chris Bridges and Patricia A. Davis

For many people, credit and credit cards are a way of life. Some use credit thoughtfully; others use credit carelessly. Because credit is such an integral part of most of our lives, it is critical that each of us learns the rules related to credit, and how to manage our credit profile so that we can obtain credit, if needed, at the lowest possible cost.

There are fees associated with the use of most types of credit —interest, late fees, excess usage fees, over the limit fees, etc. To keep from going broke paying fees, it is critical that you educate yourself about the rules related to various types of credit, and learn to play the game to win.

When credit is extended to you, you have a responsibility to repay your creditor according to the terms of the agreement you signed. To do otherwise causes a black mark on your credit record.

These black marks could strongly impact your ability to have additional credit extended to you in the future, affect your ability to get a job, cause you to be unable to rent a house or apartment, and cause you to have to pay outrageous costs for credit.

Below are a number of questions and tips related to defining credit, why one should or should not use credit, bankruptcy—what it is and when one might use it, collection agencies, the various types of credit, and more. Understanding all of this will help you in your quest to learn more about a service so many of us use, either out of necessity or for convenience.

What is a "credit report?"

MONEY TIP #22: A credit report is a document that summarizes how you handle your financial responsibilities. The reports are put together by credit reporting agencies (or credit bureaus) from information provided to them by your creditors.

A credit report provides personal and credit usage information about the consumer, such as name, address, contact number, personal details, where he/she works, social security number, marital status, descriptions of previous jobs, income, debt, and length of employment. It also contains a factual history of your credit experience with various creditors.

Although some credit reports may contain a lot of personal data, not all of it is used to evaluate your creditworthiness. For example, your marital status, employment information and income most likely will be verified another way, and not necessarily pulled from your credit report. Credit reports do not contain records of arrest, specific purchases, or medical information.

There are three main reporting agencies that compile this information and make it available to both you and to creditors with a right and a need to know. They are Equifax, Experian and TransUnion. (See Appendix C for contact information for each of the three.)

Creditors are not legally obligated to report to the credit bureaus nor do they have to report to all three. However, for the creditors who do have reporting relationships with any of the credit bureaus, you want to make sure your information is being reported accurately. By law, you are entitled to a **FREE** report once every 12 months, or more frequently, if you are denied credit based on information furnished by the specific credit bureau.

You can get access to your credit reports in several ways.

▸ Go to www.annualcreditreport.com and request a report from Experian, Equifax and TransUnion. Note: This report is free, but there is a fee for each bureau to provide your score.
▸ Call the agency or bureau directly.
▸ Visit the specific website for each agency or bureau.
▸ Get a combined report from all three credit bureaus with scores, for a nominal fee, by going online to www.getmy850.com.

Statistics have shown that over 80% of consumer credit reports have errors. To help you address these errors, the Consumer Credit Protection Act entitles you to dispute negative information on your credit report if it is inaccurate, incomplete or unverifiable. If that happens to you, then, with documentation, you can dispute the information by opening an investigation with the credit bureau(s) involved to challenge them to correct the misinformation or remove it all together.

If you challenge an entry on a credit report, always have documentation indicating payments you have made to the vendor, and your returned checks or credit card information to verify payments made. (You don't want an old account that you paid to show up at the worst time and you are forced to pay again simply because you didn't have the proper documentation.) By law, the credit bureaus have 30 days to act upon your request. If they do not, contact the Federal Trade Commission, in writing, at CRC-240; Washington, DC 20580, and ask for assistance in getting the matter resolved. It is always best to dispute in writing, and keep records of all communication to and from the credit bureau.

I have a lot of credit cards I don't use. A friend suggested I close all of those accounts because having so many cards is affecting my credit score. I think I should keep them open just in case I need them one day. Which one of us is correct?

MONEY TIP #23: You are more correct than your friend is. You should not systematically close all of the cards you are not using, but for a different reason than you indicated. However, to maximize your credit rating, develop a strategy to pay down or off any outstanding debt you have, including credit cards. You don't have to pay off all of the open cards at once to have a positive impact on your credit score. You can pay them off slowly. If you are not using some of them, cut them up; just don't close them all at one time.

Having a large number of open credit cards can look bad on your credit report and can actually lower your credit score. That's because with so many open accounts, creditors know that, at any moment, you can run up each of them to their maximum credit limit.

Your credit score is a numerical representation of your default risk on loan repayments, with a low number representing a higher risk for the lender. Scores are derived from your credit history, and range from 300 to 850. Low credit scores mean higher interest rates, inability to have certain services put in your own name (like utilities or housing), lack of consideration for certain jobs, and denial of additional credit in your name.

Closing all of the accounts you are not using at one time actually can hurt rather than help your credit score. It would be better to gradually, close some of them, starting with the newest one if you have multiple credit cards. Why? Because the length of your credit history is a key component in calculating your credit score. (See Appendix A for a description of the FICO credit scoring model.)

Also, credit bureaus look at something called your "**credit utilization ratio**," which is the percentage of the total amount of credit available to you that you are actually using. For example, suppose you have three credit cards with a limit of $1,000 each for a total of $3,000 of available credit; have outstanding charges of $500 on two of them; and nothing on the third. Your utilization ratio is 33% ($1000/$3000). If you decide to close the account with a zero balance, you are using $1,000 of the $2,000 of credit available versus $1,000 of the $3,000 you had available before you closed the account, and your utilization ratio is 50% ($1000/$2000). Doing this will negatively impact your credit score because your credit utilization ratio has gone up from 33% to 50%—17 percentage points.

Your ratio of used credit to available credit should be in the 30 percent or lower range because that shows you are using much less than half the credit available to you. Be sure to take that ratio into consideration if you start closing accounts.

My husband tells me I am not managing my money well and am abusing my credit cards. What are the signs this is the case?

MONEY TIP #24: If you are constantly buying things you don't need or can't afford, are paying only the minimum amount on credit cards, or are missing payments, then indeed, your husband may be right.

Credit is a privilege, not a right. It is extended to you based on your promise to repay any debt you incur, according to the terms and conditions of the agreement, and your history of doing so. There are several clear signs you **may** be abusing your credit cards. For instance:

- ▸ You use credit cards to pay for non-emergency items you do not need and do not have the cash to pay for.
- ▸ You use credit cards for "emergencies" because you have no other way to cover the cost.
- ▸ You have a credit card with a balance from virtually every store where you shop, despite the usually exorbitant interest rates most store cards carry.
- ▸ You only can pay the minimum payment, cannot afford to pay off the full balance during the current billing cycle, and have maxed out your cards.
- ▸ You use your credit card instead of buying something with the cash you have available at that time, and then pay only the minimum payment amount when the card comes in.
- ▸ You regularly charge an item today expecting to pay the bill with money you will have in the future.

▶ You play the balance transfer game, merely moving charges from one credit card to another, hopefully, to achieve a lower interest rate.

If you are exhibiting any of these signs, then you need to stop spending, and put your credit cards out of reach so they will not be so easily accessible. (I have been told the freezer is a good place to put them because it takes a while for them to thaw out. By then, hopefully, the urge to spend will have passed.)

Collection agencies—what are they? Do they have to be taken seriously?

MONEY TIP #25: Collection agencies are organizations your creditors use to collect money you owe them after their own attempts to get you to pay have failed. They have to be taken very seriously and are a black mark on your credit report. To avoid having a collection agency have to contact you, pay all of your creditors according to the agreed upon terms and conditions of your contracts. Work hard to avoid ever having your account go to a collection agency.

Having your account turned over to a collection agency should be taken very seriously! When an original creditor has been unsuccessful in collecting payments from a consumer, the creditor may choose to sell the debt to a third party known as a "collection agency," usually, for less than the amount of the debt. At that time, the collection agency has authority to seek payment from the consumer and will reference the original creditor on the credit report. When this occurs, the collection agency has the right to collect the full amount originally owed or accept a settlement amount for less. (They may be a different company than the one with whom you originally contracted.)

Since the collection agency purchases the debt for less than the original amount, when they offer a settlement, they are still making a profit. Therefore, settlements do not usually result in a loss to them and are advantageous to the consumer if the full amount cannot be paid. The account is then reported to the credit bureaus as either "paid," "settled for less than owed," "settled for less," or simply "settlement." This reporting implies the debt has been resolved in some manner.

One thing to note about collection reporting is that this collection account will remain on your credit report for 7 years from the last 180-day late payment on the original account, whether or not the debt has been repaid. If a collection account is paid in full, the consumer will receive a higher number of points added to the credit score than with a settlement. However, paying the collection completely will ensure an increase to the credit score versus not paying and leaving it open.

Typically, we see collection accounts for industries such as medical, utility companies, automobiles, rent, etc. Accounts in these industries are called "alternative credit accounts" because they are not reported to the credit bureaus at the time credit is established.

If it's an alternative credit account and not previously reported, then the collection will be a new "bad" account and can decrease your credit score by as much as 80 to 100 points and stays on your report for 7 years. If the account is paid in full or through a settlement, that will improve your score, but you will not get all of the points lost right away. It could take months or years for your credit score to recover from a collection account.

What are some ways to pay down debt quickly?

MONEY TIP #26: To begin, create two debt schedules: On one, list your debts in descending order of interest rate, from highest to lowest, with the balance owed beside each. Then, create another list of your debts in order of balance owed, from smallest to highest. You can pay down debt more quickly by starting with the first account on your list, and, when that debt is paid off, add that payment amount to the second entry on the list, and so on.

There are several ways to pay down debt and become financially free. The first thing to know is that there is such a thing as "good" debt. Debt is considered "good" when it is incurred to buy something that will grow in value. Examples of "good" debt are debts incurred to pay for a college education, to buy real estate, and funds to start a small business.

On the opposite side, there is "bad" debt which is incurred to buy depreciating assets. Examples of "bad" debt are debts to purchase items such as clothes and cars, and credit card debt.

There are more than 160 million Americans who have credit card debt, with average balances totaling almost $15,000. Depending on the type of this debt, credit scores may be negatively impacted by as much as 30%. Since credit card debt is considered "bad" debt, every effort should be made to pay it off as quickly as possible. You can begin by not adding more debt and simply stop using your credit cards. Just remember, do not close the accounts all at once, since doing so can negatively impact your credit score.

You can also pay down debt more quickly if you know the billing cycle and make your payment earlier in the cycle instead of waiting until the due date. This simple payment adjustment accelerates the payoff of your balances by eliminating interest that is accrued based on the average daily balance.

Another tip to pay down debt quickly is the rolling debt payment method. This is done when you pay off the first account, then you add the amount you were paying on the first account to the monthly amount you were already paying on the next account. This compounded effect increases the amount paid toward each debt as you go down your list of accounts, starting with the lowest balances first. Many financial advisors prefer this method because, from a psychological point of view, it gives the debtor encouragement to see some of the accounts paid off.

Alternatively, some people prefer to start the payoff process by paying down the debt with the highest interest rate to maximize interest savings. The procedure is the same as described above. When you have paid off the account with the highest interest rate, you, then, move to the one with the next highest interest rate, adding the amount you were paying on the first account to the monthly amount you were already paying on the next account, and so on. Using this method saves the most dollars in terms of the amount of interest paid.

What does it mean to file bankruptcy, and is it always bad?

MONEY TIP #27: Bankruptcy is a legal proceeding involving a person or business that is unable to repay outstanding debts. It is a serious mark on your credit record and has implications far into the future. Although it is not a dirty word or necessarily the result of your failure, you should enter into it cautiously and with good counsel from a bankruptcy attorney.

The bankruptcy process begins with a petition filed by the debtor or on behalf of creditors. All of the debtor's assets are measured and evaluated, whereupon the assets are used to repay a portion of outstanding debt. Upon the successful completion of bankruptcy proceedings, the debtor is relieved of the debt obligations incurred before filing for bankruptcy.

There are at least six types of bankruptcy filings available based on specific guidelines, but the two most commonly filed for by consumers are Chapter 7 and Chapter 13.

Chapter 7 of the Bankruptcy Code provides for "liquidation," (i.e., the sale of a debtor's non-exempt property and the distribution of the proceeds to creditors). After the asset sale and distribution, most remaining debts are wiped away, with a few exceptions. Any exempt property (household goods, personal belongings and usually the filer's personal residence) remains the filer's property. A Chapter 7 bankruptcy must be removed from your credit report after 10 years from the date of discharge.

Chapter 13 of the Bankruptcy Code provides for adjusting debts of an individual with a regular income. A Chapter 13 bankruptcy filing involves rehabilitating the debtor to allow them to use future earnings to pay all or part of the amount owed to creditors. This filing allows the debtor to keep his or her property and pay off debts over time, usually three to five years. A Chapter 13 bankruptcy filing must be removed from your credit report after 7 years from the date of discharge.

Although your credit score will be negatively impacted with a reported bankruptcy, after the bankruptcy is discharged, typically, you will see an increase. This improvement usually occurs after the discharge, and when new credit is established and positive reporting is maintained.

Since the law changed in 2005, it has become much more difficult for consumers to qualify for bankruptcy. In some cases, consumers who do not qualify for a Chapter 7 are redirected to file a Chapter 13 under which they will have to repay at least some of their debts. To determine whether you are eligible to file for Chapter 7 bankruptcy, the law requires you to compare your current monthly income against your state's median income for a household of your size. If your income is less than or equal to your state's median income, then you can file for Chapter 7. In other words, you have to pass a "means test" to be permitted to file for Chapter 7. ("Means test" calculators are available online by going to www.legalconsumer.com and following the directions for the "means-test" calculator for your zip code.) Bankruptcy is a serious decision and you should always seek counsel from a bankruptcy attorney before filing.

Finally, before being permitted to file either Chapter 7 or Chapter 13, filers must go through credit counseling sessions with an agency approved by the U.S. Trustee's Office, a branch of the Department of Justice. The purpose of the credit counseling is to help determine whether the filing is indeed the best way for you to handle the debt you have amassed. If a repayment plan is developed, it must be submitted to the bankruptcy court, along with a certificate of completion of the counseling session, before you will be allowed to file. A later component of the process is to have you attend financial literacy classes. Once completion has been certified and submitted to the court, then and only then will you get a bankruptcy discharge wiping out your debts.

I am looking for a loan. What is the difference between "secured" and "unsecured" credit?

MONEY TIP #28: "Secured" and "unsecured" loans are different types of credit, but both represent a commitment you make to a lender to repay under agreed upon terms and conditions.

"Secured" loans are usually for big-ticket items like a house, car or boat and have a title associated with them with the lender's name listed as the official owner of record. "Unsecured" loans have no title and are most often associated with credit cards.

The two types of credit are decidedly different. "Secured" credit is a type of credit where you buy something of value that is then used to guarantee repayment, like a car, house or boat. There is a title associated with this type of credit, and the lender is listed on the title as the lien holder. It is impossible for you to sell or pledge a secured item until the lien holder signs over the title to you. "Secured" loans are loans for specific assets that can be taken back (repossessed) by the lender if you fail to pay. If that happens, you no longer will be able to use the assets until (or unless) you bring the loan current. Also, expect slow or non-payment to negatively affect your credit rating.

"Unsecured" credit does not require something tangible to guarantee the loan and is extended totally based on the consumer's creditworthiness. Credit cards and personal loans are examples of this type of credit. The lender usually does not repossess items bought using "unsecured" credit. However, these types of accounts may be subject to collection through a law suit.

Is it true that there are no advantages to using credit and if I can't pay cash for my purchase, then I cannot afford it?

MONEY TIP #29: No, this is not true. There are many advantages of using credit, and they are listed below. If you have to pay for the purchase over an extended period of time, and pay only the minimum monthly payment, unless it is an emergency

or is for a big-ticket item, consider holding off on the purchase until you have more available cash. If you must make the purchase, consider a less expensive option that is more affordable.

That one must not be able to afford a purchase if you can't pay cash is a commonly held belief that is not true. Plus, there are a number of advantages of using credit, as long as you use it wisely.

- ▸ Credit can be useful in times of emergency if you don't have the money to pay in full for the item.
- ▸ Credit can be more convenient than cash.
- ▸ Some merchants, such as rental car companies and hotels, often require you to provide a credit card number to be able to use their services. Also, some airlines now require a credit card for on-board purchases, including food and drinks.
- ▸ The use of credit can make it possible/easier to make large purchases such as a car, house or major appliance, if the cash is not available.
- ▸ Using credit can earn you rewards or miles that can be used for things like future purchases, dining out, travel, and bill payment.
- ▸ Credit is often safer than cash. With a credit card, under the law, your liability is limited if a loss is reported timely. Cash can be lost or stolen with little chance that it will be recovered or replaced.
- ▸ If there is a problem with an item purchased with a credit card, the card issuer often will help you resolve any dispute with the merchant, and may withhold the release of payment to the merchant until the matter has been resolved.
- ▸ Many credit card issuers offer a cash rebate of up to five percent of the amount purchased.

To incur the least overall cost, pay the credit card bill in its entirety by the due date, if possible. That way, you will have had the use of the creditor's money for the length of the "grace period" and it has not cost you any interest.   (The "grace period" is the time between your actual purchase and the payment due date.)

Credit is a great way to pay for things I want but can't afford right now. Are there any disadvantages to using credit?

MONEY TIP #30: Yes, credit is a way to pay for things you may not have the cash now to pay for. And, yes, there are many disadvantages to using credit, especially if you abuse the privilege. As long as you use credit wisely and make timely payments, there should not be any problems.

There is nothing to be ashamed of if you do not have cash readily available to pay for a purchase. Credit is an alternative that can be used as long as it is used carefully and always repaid according to the terms of your agreement with the lender.

As mentioned, there are many disadvantages to using credit, especially if you don't use it wisely. Here are a few:

▸ Credit costs money. Some creditors charge high interest rates when a balance is carried over from one month to the next. I am aware of rates as high as a whopping 32.99 percent! That means for every $100 you buy using credit, at that rate, you owe $132.99!

▸ The use of credit may tempt you to overspend. (Statistics show that consumers often spend as much as one-third more on purchases made on credit than for a similar item paid for with cash.)

▸ Credit commits the use of tomorrow's income to repay today's debts.   (If you will have the money "tomorrow," this is not necessarily bad.)

▸ Lenders report missed payments to credit bureaus, causing a lower credit score.

▸ Select items purchased may be repossessed if payments are missed.

▸ If the debt is not repaid on time, it may affect your ability to get a job, a residence or additional credit.   Companies may not want to hire you and mortgage companies may not want to lend you money if you are deeply in debt, as you may be considered a high risk.

Again, if you must use credit to buy something that you will finance over an extended period of time, incur hefty interest rates for, or even have to pay added penalties, if it is not an emergency, you may want to do without the item or wait until you can pay cash for it. Also, consider an alternative that is less costly. (Remember my husband, Jim Davis' adage, "Work for it; wait for it; and pay for it.")

Exceptions may be what we call "big ticket items" such as a house, a car or a boat. Typically, these are items most of us are unable to pay for with cash. Make sure, for these purchases, you negotiate the best possible deal for yourself, including both the price and the cost of financing the item.

A participant in one of my classes admitted having an especially bad credit history. She was in the market for a used car, but was having trouble finding a willing lender. Finally, she found both—a nine-year-old car, and a willing lender, but at a very high cost. The quoted interest rate was a whopping 24 percent for 7 years! She asked what she should do. My recommendation? BMW–Bus, Metro or Walk! (The class laughed heartily when they realized I didn't mean the car—BMW.) She ended up not taking the deal. That was an exorbitant interest rate, and the seven-year term probably was longer than the life expectancy of the used car she was considering.

Another student was very upset because her poor credit history was hampering her ability to get a job. She had received three job offers, but each had been withdrawn after the potential employer examined her credit report. She was applying for a job as a security officer. She stated, wearily, "Just because I'm broke, doesn't mean I'm a crook." No, but given a choice between two candidates, the employers decided to go with candidates whose need for money was not so obvious. Hopefully, these disappointments caused her to work hard on getting her finances straight.

If I have no debt and never have, does that mean my credit is good?

MONEY TIP #31: No, it does not; quite the contrary. With no credit history, potential creditors don't have any way of knowing you and how you handle credit. To establish credit, consider opening an account in your name, using it responsibly, and re-paying the debt according to the agreed terms. This will help show potential creditors that you are a reliable debtor.

Not having a credit history may not be as great an idea as you think. For lenders to assess whether you use credit responsibly, you must show evidence of having had credit extended to you, and of having lived up to the "Terms and Conditions" of your contractual agreements. Thus, because you have never had credit, you may be denied the credit you seek. In addition to opening up your own credit account, another way to establish credit is to be added to someone else's account as an authorized user.

If my credit is bad, can I pay someone to "fix" my credit and remove all negative information from my credit report?

MONEY TIP #32: No, you cannot; not legally. If you need help, there are several organizations you can contact that have no motive other than to help you work through your financial distress. The National Foundation for Credit Counseling (NFCC), one of the largest non-profit credit counseling organizations in the country, is one such entity. It offers consumers both financial education and counseling services. Their web address is www.nfcc.org. Another is Operation Hope, Inc. (HOPE), a provider of financial literacy and economic empowerment programs. HOPE has developed a series of programs to provide free financial education to youths and adults nationwide. Go to each organization's website for a listing of offices in your area.

Being able to pay someone to "fix" one's credit is a myth that is quite widespread, but has no basis in fact. The following are universal truths about credit repair:

- ▶ No one can have accurate information removed from your credit report, not even you!
- ▶ If you have had credit problems in the past, it can take years to repair your credit, legitimately.
- ▶ No one can create a new identity for you unless you have been a victim of severe identity theft, and it is difficult even under those circumstances. Each of us gets only one

Social Security number. Even if someone offers to get an EIN (employer identification number) for you, it is tied to your Social Security number. Plus, under the credit repair statutes, changing your identity to avoid debt repayment is against the law.

▸ You can order your own credit report. You are legally entitled to one free credit report a year from each of the three major credit bureaus listed in Appendix C. (Consider ordering one every four months from a different agency to have a general idea, all year, about what is in your credit report.) If you see errors on your credit report, you can submit the supporting documentation to the credit bureau yourself and request the appropriate corrections be made. By law, the agencies have 30 days to remove negative information when they receive documentation that clearly indicates that the information on your credit report is incorrect. If they do not cooperate, you may submit a written complaint to the Federal Trade Commission in Washington, D.C. (See Appendix C for the address.)

Some credit repair companies are legitimate. Many are not. Most do nothing for you that you cannot do for yourself. You can call creditors to renegotiate payment schedules and try to get lower credit payoff amounts. (Be wary of any credit-related entity that advertises on trees, stop signs or traffic signals. Legitimate businesses do not advertise that way!)

If you are really "broke" and unable to make payments on your credit cards, **DO NOT** fall for the catchy television ads that tell you that you don't have to pay your credit card companies—to just call them (the advertiser). They claim they can help you avoid payment.

There is no longer a debtor's prison to punish people who refuse to pay debts. If you incurred the debt without breaking any laws, legally, you can stop paying it at any time. However, be aware that doing so not only will **severely** damage your credit, but can lead to a number of other undesirable actions, such as:

▸ Your wages can be garnished.

▸ There likely will be many collection letters and phone calls to your home or place of employment.

▸ You can be sued and a judgment placed on your credit report. Judgments are one of the worst items to have on your credit report. They signify you do not live up to the agreed upon terms and conditions of any contract you sign. Judgements are a flashing neon sign to a potential creditor that says, "BEWARE!" They can prevent you from being granted credit for any purchases or services, especially, essential ones, such as a car, home, apartment, utilities or major appliances.

If I co-sign for a loan for a friend or family member and they fail to repay the loan according to the terms of the agreement, will I be held responsible for the unpaid balance?

MONEY TIP #33: Yes, you will. For that reason, never co-sign for any loan you are not able and willing to repay. Treat any loan as though you were borrowing the money yourself.

You will be held responsible because you signed your name on the loan documents. Remember, your friend or relative has asked you to co-sign because, based upon their stand-alone credit record, they have been denied credit. If a professional lender has turned your friend or relative down, consider it probably is for good reason and is something you should not take lightly. (Ask yourself why you think they will repay this loan—in both your names—in a timely fashion, if they did not pay back money borrowed in their name alone.)

In almost all states, if the borrower misses a payment, by law, the lender immediately can (and usually will) turn to the co-signer without even trying to collect from the borrower. Such a delinquency negatively affects your credit rating just as though you were the original borrower and shows up as a liability on your credit record. This could prevent you from getting credit for yourself in the future. In addition to being required to bring the payments current, you could be assessed late fees, have your wages garnished, be sued, and even be assessed legal fees.

Despite the risks above, there still may come a time when you want to or have to co-sign for a loan. Perhaps one of your children, a close friend or a family member needs help in establishing credit or has an emergency situation. Just make sure you do the following before you co-sign:

▸ Be certain you can afford to repay the loan, if needed.
▸ Be aware your own credit rating may be affected if the loan goes into default.
▸ Recognize you may be prohibited from getting credit approved for yourself because of having your name on that outstanding loan.
▸ Understand that, if sued because of a default, you may lose some of your own valuable items as the lender tries to collect.
▸ Completely read the loan documents (and get a copy).
▸ Fully comprehend your duties and rights as a co-signer.

Remember, adding your name to someone else's debt is taking on a very serious financial responsibility. If the lender did not have doubts about the borrower's ability or willingness to repay the loan, no co-signer would have been required. Remember these two old adages:

- ▶ Don't co-sign away your good credit!
- ▶ Look deep before you leap!

I need a relatively small amount of money quickly and can't find a regular lender to make me a loan. Since I can prove I have a job, can't I just go to a "payday lender" or to a "title loan" company and get the same terms I would get from a bank or credit union, just more quickly?

MONEY TIP #34: Absolutely, not! Do everything you can to avoid these types of loans, and find another source for your short-term cash needs. (Some call the makers of these loans "predatory lenders.") Typically, banks and credit unions offer rates that are much lower than those of payday and title lenders. Try these alternatives before seeking out the more expensive ones.

"Payday lenders" are lenders who charge exorbitant fees to people who need money quickly and can't get a loan from a more mainstream lender like a bank or credit union. Their only two requirements are that you have a job and a checking account. These lenders advance you money, theoretically, until your next payday. (Statistics say the average payday loan turns over seven times before it is closed out.)

Here is how these loans work. The payday lender writes you a check for the amount of the loan. You give the lender a check written on your checking account for the amount of the loan, plus fees which typically run as much as 30% for two weeks. The lender then holds your check until your next payday at which time, by agreement, your check is deposited or cashed. Statistics show the average payday loan is renewed seven times with just the interest being paid (not the principal amount borrowed), and can result in interest rates of 300 percent or higher, plus fees!

A real-life example:

This former client is single, childless and makes $85,000 per year. Her expenses were so far out of proportion to her income that she regularly used payday loans to provide her spending money. When we met, she had five of them. Three were for $300; one was for $250; and one was for $350, for a total of $1,500—all with different payday lenders. Every payday, she merely paid each lender a 30 percent fee ($450 in total) and rolled over the principal amounts. Most of her lenders would not accept partial repayment of the principal. So, unless she had the entire amount, some would only accept the interest and another two-week loan agreement. She rolled these loans over six times. By the time she was done, she had paid the $450 fee 6 times, plus the principal amount, for a total of $4,200 to borrow $1,500 for about 12 weeks!

Similarly, title loans are another source for those who need quick money. These loans are made to people who can prove they are the registered owner of a vehicle that has no loan on it. The lenders who work in this arena will lend you up to 50 percent of the Black Book value of your car. (The Black Book value is the auction value and is much less than the Blue Book value.) These lenders want to be able to sell your car quickly and still come out whole, should you default on the loan. When you go to this type of lender, there are three requirements: 1) you must have a clean and clear title; 2) all owners listed on the title must come in and sign over the title; and 3) you must bring a spare key! The latter allows the lender to repossess your car easily if you do not repay the loan. Their rates are almost as high as those of the payday lenders mentioned above.

CHAPTER 5

Surviving Job Loss
What to Do When the Paycheck Stops

Losing a job no longer has the stigma associated with it that it once did. Today, thousands of people lose jobs as companies, big and small, merge, get sold, downsize, "right-size," go out of business, and more.

If you are one who has lost a job, or expects to soon, the challenge is to look for new employment while simultaneously "keeping the home fires burning." Your time and energy have to be divided between an active job search and modified spending to stretch your resources until you are able to find a new job. Remember, not having your dream job doesn't mean you have to be "broke." There are loads of ways to earn money, in the interim, and keep a roof over your head. You just have to find them and be willing to do them.

There are many ways to do both of these. This chapter offers several tips for doing so.

I have just lost my job and I'm starting to panic. What steps should I follow to try to take control of this new situation?

MONEY TIP #35: Put off or reduce any unnecessary spending until you get a firm handle on the new situation and have made a plan for going forward. Then, take the other steps listed below.

The loss of a job can be devastating. Don't blame yourself. That's a waste of time and energy. Most of all, don't panic. Instead, spend time developing a plan to get yourself and your family stable until you find another job.

Getting control of your finances is a must. Below are some early steps to take to help ease the pain, lessen the panic, and begin to gain control over the situation:

- ▶ Stop all non-essential spending.
- ▶ File for unemployment insurance. You should take this step immediately upon finding out about your job loss. The application can be done either online or via phone. Google "unemployment application" for your state or county contact information. (Rules vary by state and county.)
- ▶ Check with your human resources office to see if there are any company benefits available to help carry you through this time, such as severance; payment for any accumulated leave; COBRA benefits which allow continuation of medical coverage for up to 18 months; and outplacement services.

- ▶ Talk to your immediate family members about the new situation and enlist their help to re-prioritize family needs and wants. Find out what they can do to help during this transition period.

- ▶ Develop a family spending plan that reflects these priorities and strips away any excess. (See Chapter 2.)

- ▶ List your assets, so you can see what resources you have available.

- ▶ List all your creditors (name, address, phone number, contact, amount owed, minimum balance, and interest rate).

- ▶ Notify your creditors of your change in status, and work out a new payment schedule with them, if they will.

- ▶ Stay in touch with your creditors to keep them fully engaged.

- ▶ If you belong to a union, check with your union representative to determine what, if any, benefits you may be eligible for.

I don't know which bills I should pay first. How do I prioritize?

MONEY TIP #36: You must first pay the bills critical to your family's housing, utility and health needs. Money for food also should be a priority.

When you don't have enough money to pay all of your bills, you have to make some hard, well-thought-out decisions. First, itemize all your outstanding bills by going through your checkbook and payment books to make sure you have all of them. Then, rearrange these bills, in priority order.

Your most important expenses to allocate money to are:

1. Rent/mortgage
2. Utilities
3. Health insurance
4. Food
5. Car payment
6. Car insurance
7. Child support
8. Alimony
9. Student loans

If there is money left over, then look at your other debts, like store and merchant debt. You may consider paying those with the highest interest rate first since that saves you the most money.

Be sure to contact your creditors to explain your situation, if you need to negotiate new payment terms. Be mindful that missed payments to any of them are likely to be reflected on your credit report and result in a lower credit score.

Since I don't have enough money to pay all my bills, shouldn't I just ignore all bill collectors and try to catch up when I get another job?

MONEY TIP #37: No. The absolute worst thing you could do would be to ignore communications from your creditors. Instead, you should proactively contact every creditor, explain the situation, and try to work out a revised payment plan.

After you have contacted your lenders, follow up any telephone calls with a letter or email summarizing the discussion so you have a record for your files. The communication should include the date and your name, address, email address, and account number.

Keep copies of any written communications to creditors (as well as the reply) in a labeled file or a secured email folder, with the name, phone number and title of the contact.

Can't I just live off of my credit cards, and, then, pay those bills when I am employed again?

MONEY TIP #38: No, you cannot. Remember, the first step you must take when you lose your job, is, "Stop non-essential spending!" You must figure out a way to reduce your spending to a point where you are living within whatever resources you and your family can put together.

The "buy now/pay later" approach is not a good one in this type of situation. You should immediately reach out to every creditor, explain the job loss and try to negotiate a more favorable payment plan—one you know you can honor, even during your unemployment. (Your credit score might take a hit, but you must be up front with your creditors.)

As is discussed in Money Tip #39 below, when you have limited resources, you must learn to live on less. Maintaining your old standard of living today and paying for it tomorrow only means you'll be that much further behind when you do get a job. You will have to use all of your initial paychecks from the new job to fund the "above your means" lifestyle you lived while you were unemployed.

In Money Tip #40, there is a discussion of the other side of the coin—how to generate more income. Listed there are a number of creative ways for you to generate cash to help cover your paycheck-free lifestyle. You just have to be willing to work at jobs below your skill level, temporarily, until you can find one more in line with your talents.

Can you give me some ideas on how to live on less, even if it is only temporary?

MONEY TIP #39: Yes. Become extremely frugal; be a more-informed and creative consumer; shop in lower-cost stores; and cut out name brands.

Learning how to live on less may not be easy, but it is something you must figure out how to do. It takes focus, determination, family cooperation, and a willingness to do things differently.

There are a number of things you can do before you spend money. They will help you determine whether you can do without and/or whether there is another way to get what you want other than spending scarce dollars and still have your needs met.

- ▶ Determine whether the item is a want or a need. If it is a want, then postpone the purchase or do without, at least, for now.
- ▶ Determine whether you can make a product rather than buy it.
- ▶ Buy items second hand.
- ▶ Barter /trade for goods and services.
- ▶ Buy needed clothing either on sale or at discount stores.
- ▶ Take nearly-new clothes to a consignment shop to sell.
- ▶ Determine whether you have a skill that can be used to generate money, such as sewing, cooking, or handyman work.

- ▸ Use grocery coupons when you shop.
- ▸ Join loyalty programs in stores you frequent.
- ▸ Make a shopping list when you go to the store and restrict yourself to buying only items on the list.
- ▸ Use generic or store brands, where available.
- ▸ Wrap and store foods carefully to prolong their freshness and cut back on waste.
- ▸ If there are multiple cars in the family, try to get by with at least one less car to save on the cost of maintenance and insurance (and maybe even the car payment itself).
- ▸ Comparison shop in your neighborhood for gasoline.
- ▸ Plan errands efficiently to cut back on gas usage.
- ▸ Switch to a higher deductible to reduce your auto insurance premium.
- ▸ Bundle all your insurance coverage with one company to take advantage of discounts offered by having multiple policies with them.
- ▸ Consider liability coverage only on any cars you own that do not have significant value.
- ▸ Review both your phone and cable bills, and eliminate any services you can do without.
- ▸ Take on a roommate to lower your monthly housing cost.
- ▸ Price and install water-saver showerheads to cut back on water and energy.
- ▸ Schedule a free utility audit of your home to check for leaks in areas where insulation might provide savings on your energy bill.
- ▸ Turn off lights and appliances when they are not being used.
- ▸ Consider having a garage sale to get rid of items no longer needed.
- ▸ Check out books, magazines, and movies from the library rather than buy them.

I really am broke, and it's no fun. Can you give me some ideas about ways to earn money until I can find another job in my profession?

MONEY TIP #40: Get creative about your own talents and the extent to which they can be used to generate revenue. Also, be willing to expand your horizons and do some jobs you never imagined you could or would do. Have the strong conviction that you and your family will survive this temporary setback.

Following are some things you might try to generate cash until you find the job you want.

▶ Sell unused gift cards.

▶ Become a babysitter, house sitter, or pet sitter.

▶ Become a dog walker. On the PeerRenters app, go to "list" then to "Personal Services" to find opportunities.

▶ Do random chores for neighbors and friends.

▶ Sell old CDs, DVDs and electronics.

▶ Cook, clean, or sew for friends and family.

▶ Return unused/unworn items with tags.

▶ Sell old books to a local used bookstore.

▶ Become a film extra. Go to CraigsList and search for "film extras."

▶ Upload your digital images for resale on a website like www.Imaginairie.com.

▶ Become a mystery shopper. Google "mystery shopper" and also check out Mystery Shoppers Providers Association.

▶ Join a focus group. Go to CraigsList and search for "jobs and gigs;" then click on "focus groups."

- Become a website tester. Try sites like StartUpLift, Userlytics, and UserTesting.
- Become an Uber or Lyft driver.
- Advertise on your car. ("It's called Car Wrapping.") Go to the website www.Wrapify.com.
- Get paid to take surveys. Pinecone Research, Toluna, Global Test Market, Ipsos I-Say, Opinion Outpost, MySurvey, and SurveySpot are a few you might check out.
- Get paid by Concepts Consumer Research to test products.

So, you see, there are lots of opportunities for you to become "un-broke." Go for it!

It's been a while since I last had to look for a job. Where can I look for job listings other than my local newspaper?

MONEY TIP #41: There are many local job sites available. Try them, but also put the word out to your network of friends, neighbors, and associates that you are in the job market, and don't be afraid to ask for their help.

Some other places to look for leads in your job search include:

I. CareerOneStop
    Sponsored by the U.S. Department of Labor, CareerOneStop lists hundreds of thousands of jobs. It also links to employment and training programs in each state, including programs for people with disabilities, minorities, older workers, veterans, welfare recipients,

and youth. For federal jobs, all open federal positions are announced to the public on usajobs.gov.

2. **State and county offices**

   Your state's Department of Labor may have job listings or be able to point you to local job offices that offer counseling and referrals. Local and county human resources offices provide some placement assistance, too. They can give you the names of other groups that may be helpful, like labor unions or federally-funded vocational programs.

3. **College career and alumni service offices**

   Contact local college placement offices to determine what help they may be able to offer. If you're not a current student or an alum, some still may permit you access to their job listings.

4. **Local libraries**

   Ask the librarian to point you to information on such things as writing a resume, interviewing, and compiling a list of companies and organizations to contact about job openings.

5. **Online job boards**

   Check out job listings on sites like Monster.com, ZipRecruiter.com, and CareerBuilder.com.

6. **Job fairs**

   Job fairs are large meetings where organizations seeking workers provide information about job vacancies, and job seekers provide resumes and information about their qualifications for those jobs. Employers, colleges and universities, government agencies, and professional organizations are but a few of the types of organizations that host job fairs. The resources listed above will often have information about upcoming job fairs.

I am desperate to find a job and some announcements sound "too good to be true." How can I tell "real" ones from those that are fake?

MONEY TIP #42: When you start your job search, begin by using only "free" job sites. This is not the time to expend resources you do not have. These sites are far less likely to be scams. Should the search become extended and you want to use a fee-based organization, investigate them fully before giving them any money.

Scammers advertise jobs the same places legitimate employers do—online, in newspapers, and even on TV and radio. Here are some ways to tell whether a job lead may be a scam:

1. **You need to pay to get the job.**
    They may say they've got a job waiting or guarantee to place you in a job if you just pay a fee for certification, training materials, or their expenses placing you with a company. But, after you pay, the job doesn't materialize. Employers and employment firms shouldn't ask you to pay for the promise of a job.

2. **You are asked to supply your credit card or bank account information.**
    Don't give out your credit card or bank account information over the phone to a company unless you're familiar with them and have agreed to pay for something. Anyone who has your account information can use it.

3. **The ad is for "previously undisclosed" federal government jobs.**

Information about available federal jobs is free. And all federal positions are announced to the public on www. usajobs.gov. Don't believe anyone who promises you a federal or postal job.

4. **The ad is from a job placement service.**
    Many job placement services are legitimate, especially those offered for free by federal, county and local governments. (Given your limited resources, check these out first.)

    But, some others are not truthful about what they'll do for you; promote outdated or fake job openings; or charge up-front fees for services that may not lead to a job. In fact, they might not even return your calls once you pay.

    Before you decide to enlist a private company's help:

    a.) Check with the hiring company.
         If a company or organization is mentioned in an ad or interview, contact that company to find out if the company really is hiring through the service.

    b.) Get details in writing.
         Ask what the cost is; what you will get; and who pays—you or the company that hires you. Also, you want to know what happens if the service doesn't find a job for you or provide you with any real leads. If they are reluctant to answer your questions, or give confusing answers, you should hesitate to work with them.

         Get a copy of the contract with the placement firm and read it carefully. A legitimate company will give you time to read the contract and decide, not pressure you into signing immediately. Make sure any promises—including refund promises—are in writing. Some listing services and "consultants" write ads to sound like jobs, but that's just a marketing trick. They are really selling general information about getting a job—information you can find for free on your own.

c.) Know whether it's job placement or job counseling.

Executive or career counseling services help people with career directions and decisions. They may offer services like skills identification and self-evaluation, resume preparation, letter writing, interview techniques, and general information about companies or organizations in a particular location or job field. But, job placement isn't guaranteed. Fees can be as high as thousands of dollars, and you often have to pay in advance.

We have two adult children who are always asking us for money. Now, my spouse has lost his job and we are looking for places to cut back. I feel the kids should be cut off; my spouse doesn't. What do you think?

MONEY TIP #43: Now is not the time to give your adult children money you don't have. Instead, give them something that ultimately will be more valuable and lasting—give them the gift of financial literacy to educate them on ways to better manage their resources to be able to take care of themselves and their families without depending on mom and dad.

A 2015 survey from the Pew Research Center of nearly 1,700 Americans found 61% of parents with grown children had helped them out financially in the past year. Most of the parents didn't consider this a burden. Almost 72% felt they were expected to help their children, and 89% found it rewarding to be able to do so. You don't say how much you usually give each of them, but, the U.S. Department of Agriculture reported in 2015, a middle-income family spent an average of $13,000+ per year on each adult offspring.

With your husband's recent job loss, your financial situation has changed. You and your spouse have to ask yourselves, given your limited resources now, "Can we "afford" to continue helping to support our adult children?" A "No!" answer has nothing to do with how much you love them. It means you have taken a realistic look at your own current financial situation and decided that, right now, you don't have money to spare. Also, you are not doing them any favors by always bailing them out.

This might also be a perfect time to broaden the discussion and ask why they continue to be unable to live within their means and to need regular handouts from the "Bank of Mom and Dad." You should consider offering either to help them make a spending plan or to suggest a financial advisor who can help them chart a more independent course.

There are non-financial tips and suggestions you might make that these adult children can do to ease their own financial burden. Some of the types of things suggested in Money Tip #39 above as a way of living on less are things they, too, can do to help stretch their own resources. In addition to those, you can do the following:

▸ Introduce them to coupon websites such as www.ebizma. com/articles/coupon-websites.
▸ Advise them to cook more meals at home to cut down on the cost of eating out.

- ▸ Suggest that they consider part-time employment, even if they already have a full-time job.
- ▸ Also, suggest that they give more thoughtful, less expensive, and more creative gifts.
- ▸ Encourage them to look for free entertainment for themselves and their children.
- ▸ Implementing many of these cost-saving techniques should free up enough of their own resources to operate independently from you.

CHAPTER 6

Managing Student Loans
Ways to Lighten Your Debt Load

The high cost of college has exacted a tremendous toll on our nation's young people. At the end of the second quarter of 2016, according to the Federal Reserve, 44.2 million borrowers (federal and private combined) owed a staggering $1.44 trillion! Today, 70% of college students graduate with an average debt load of $37,710—up 6% from last year.

Re-paying student loans is a burden for many borrowers, and defaults continue to rise at an alarming rate. According to the Department of Education, student loan debt losses are mounting as more and more borrowers fall behind on their payments. As of mid-2016, 11.2% of student loans were delinquent by 90+ days.

It isn't just students who are saddled with this debt. More and more parents and grandparents have co-signed on loans to help pay for their young adult loved one's college education. These co-signers end up on the hook if their children/grandchildren are unable to (or refuse to) pay the loan back. Almost 80% of the private loans that were refinanced or consolidated by the seven largest lenders, in the most recent academic year, had co-signers. According to Measure One, a company that provides analytics for the student loan industry, most often, the co-signers were the parents or grandparents of the student borrower.

If your student needs help, consider offering advice, not cash. If you immediately come to their rescue, you will miss out on the opportunity to teach them how to work through their own difficult financial situations. You can offer your own help to put together a spending plan with the aim of reducing this debt. If that help is not welcome, then they can go online and use one of the budget sites to create a workable spending plan by themselves. Another suggestion is for them to use the sample in Appendix B and create one on their own.

No one wants to go broke repaying student loan debt—not the student and certainly not his/her parents or grandparents. The objective of this chapter is to take a look at ways of managing significant student debt in a way that will lighten the load for everybody.

My daughter has almost $50,000 of college debt. What can be done to help ease that burden?

MONEY TIP #44: To ease her burden, for her federal loans, have your daughter investigate the federal programs aimed at reducing her monthly payments and loan forgiveness programs. In some cases, her repayment term can be extended and in others, depending upon the program, all or part of her loan may be eliminated.

There are several specific ways to lighten her debt load:

1. To reduce the monthly payment amount, look into one of the federal-government-mandated income driven repayment plans. These plans set the required monthly payment as a percentage of the borrower's discretionary income (the amount they make that falls above the federal poverty level), instead of their debt load, and the date of the loans. Such a plan may be applicable if your daughter's outstanding federal student loan debt is higher than or is a significant portion of her annual income.

    There are three different types of these plans, and most **federal** student loans are eligible for at least one of them. They have different eligibility requirements, payment amounts, and payback periods. At least one of them, the IBR Plan described below, has a loan forgiveness component. The plans are:

    - ▸ Income-Based Repayment Plan (IBR Plan)
    - ▸ Pay As You Earn Repayment Plan (Pay As You Earn Plan)
    - ▸ Income-Contingent Repayment Plan (ICR Plan)

    The chart on the following page shows how payment amounts are determined under each income-driven plan. Depending on her income and family size, she may have no monthly payment at all.

INCOME-DRIVEN REPAYMENT PLAN	PAYMENT AMOUNT
IBR Plan for those borrowers whose loans are dated on or before July 1, 2014	Generally, 15 percent of one's discretionary income, but less than or equal to the 10-year standard repayment plan amount. **Repayment period is 25 years.**
IBR Plan for those borrowers whose loans are dated after July 1, 2014	Generally, less than 15 percent of one's discretionary income, but less than or equal to the 10-year standard repayment plan amount. **Repayment period is 20 years.**
Pay As You Earn Plan	Generally, 10 percent of one's discretionary income, but less than or equal to the 10-year standard repayment plan amount. **Repayment period is 20 years.**
ICR Plan	The lesser of the following: 1. 20 % percent of one's discretionary income; or 2. the amount one would pay on a repayment plan with a fixed payment of 12 years, adjusted according to one's income. **Repayment period is 25 years.**

For more information and to determine which plan works best for you and your daughter's situation, go to the Department of Education's Student Aid website at www.studentaid.ed.gov/repay-loans/understand/plans/income-driven.

2.   To actually get rid of some of her student debt, see whether your daughter qualifies for one of the student loan forgiveness programs. The Student Loan Forgiveness Act (the Act), passed in 2012, provides several ways borrowers can have their federal student loans forgiven through a

variety of government programs. At the end of the day, in some programs, borrowers end up debt free! Below are several ways of partial or complete loan forgiveness allowed by the Act.

▶ **Become a public-school teacher in a low-income area.**
Under the government's Teacher Forgiveness Program, up to $17,500 of one's federal Stafford loans or the entirety of one's Perkins loans can be forgiven in exchange for five consecutive, full-time years as a teacher at certain low-income elementary or secondary schools.

▶ **Join the military.**
Each military branch has its own student loan forgiveness program. Forgiven loan amounts usually depend on the level of rank achieved. Before signing up, your daughter should contact her preferred branch to learn about how that branch's program works.

I know of a 22-year-old who just graduated from college with $35,000 worth of student debt and wants to be a nurse. After exploring many options available to her, she has just been accepted into the Navy Nursing Corps where she will be able to get the training needed to achieve her dream, paid for by the Navy. She also will be eligible to receive some loan forgiveness.

▶ **Participate in the Income-Based Repayment Plan (IBR) described above.**
The IBR adjusts students' monthly loan payments to be no more than 15% of their "discretionary" income.

For example, suppose your daughter makes $20,000 annually. Because the federal poverty level within the contiguous U.S. is $12,060 for 2016, that means she only has $8,940 of discretionary income. Under the IBR, she would only have to make payments that were 15% of that $8,940, which equals about $120 a month. (It's possible that some recent graduates make so little that they qualify to make $0 in monthly payments.) After 25 years of making these adjusted loan payments, her remaining balance will be completely forgiven.

▸ **Get a public service, government or non-profit job.**
If she borrowed money under the William D. Ford Federal Direct Loan program, she can apply to the **Public Service Loan Forgiveness Program.** In this program, full-time employees in the public service or non-profit sectors can have the remainder of their outstanding debt forgiven after they successfully make 120 qualified loan payments. To receive forgiveness, she must remain with a qualifying employer at the time she applies for and receives forgiveness for her loans.

What kinds of jobs qualify as public service? Any employment with a federal, state or local government agency, entity, or organization, or a 501(c)(3) not-for-profit organization qualifies.

Also, in return for volunteer service, AmeriCorps provides funds to repay student loan debts and the Peace Corps offers partial debt cancellation. Similarly, the Nurse Corps' Loan Repayment Program allows nurses working in "critical shortage facilities" to reduce their student loans by up to 60%. These are all viable options for students with limited resources and large debts.

▸ **Consolidate all direct student loans into one loan with a fixed interest rate.**
That way, rather than making several payments each month—a separate one for each loan—she can make one

payment and will only have a single loan servicer with which to deal. That alone can result in lower payments. (Federal and private loans shouldn't be consolidated because private lenders don't have the same repayment options permitted by federal loans.)

▶ **Try to refinance her outstanding loans to get a lower rate.**

▶ **For federal consolidated loans, extend the repayment period from the standard 10 years up to the maximum allowable 30 years, depending upon the amount of debt owed.** Borrowers who owe at least $20,000 can extend their payments to 20 years whereas those who owe at least $60,000 can extend the repayment period up to 30 years. (Given the amount of her debt, if her loans have been consolidated already, looks like she qualifies for the 20-year repayment period refinance option.) Understand that, with the extension, although the monthly payments are lower, the total amount of interest paid will be greater, even though the rate remains the same.

▶ **If her federal loans have not been consolidated, since her outstanding debt exceeds $30,000, she may be able to extend the repayment period to 25 years.**
Again, with the extension, monthly payments will be lower but, even with no change in the interest rate, the total amount of interest paid will be significantly greater.

▶ **Try to negotiate a longer repayment period, if there are any private loans.**
These repayment periods vary, depending on the lender, and range from 5 to 15 years. However, private lenders are under no obligation to allow extensions.

Given the large amount of non-federal loans I have,
I need private loan forgiveness. Is there any way to
make that happen?

MONEY TIP #45: Perhaps. Contact each of your private lenders and try to renegotiate payment terms more in line with what you believe you can reasonably pay. In addition, look into loan consolidation and/or refinance of your outstanding loans.

You are not alone. At the end of 2015, total private student loan debt reached a staggering $7.9 billion! While some repayment plans may be made available to you, private student loans often have higher interest rates than federal student loans. There are no private loan forgiveness plans; but, don't despair. There still are a few things you can try.

1. Talk to your lender. (This may be the most effective.)
2. Consolidate and refinance your private loans. (You may be able to lower your monthly payment if you refinance at a lower rate.)
3. Find a job that pays more money or add a part-time job. Doing this will provide additional resources from which to make your loan payments.

Hopefully, some combination of the above will help you lighten your load and make the payback easier.

My child can't afford student loan payments, credit card payments and his daily living expenses. Should we bite the bullet and allow him to move back home?

MONEY TIP #46: If you feel you can afford it, you might help out by paying off his credit cards and having him use all of his resources to lighten his student debt load. Also, work with him to set up a stringent spending plan aimed at launching him onto his road to financial independence.

If your child is willing to agree with the parameters you set, then having him move back home could work. Not only should there be agreements about "house rules," but also you should require the rent your child is saving be used to either pay down student loan or credit card debt (if you don't pay it yourself). You might even go so far as to set a limit on how long his "free ride" of living at home, rent-free, lasts.

I want to put aside money for college for my grand-kids, but I am afraid I might need the money down the road. Are there options?

MONEY TIP #47: Yes. To help with college expenses for your grandchildren, but to have the flexibility to access the funds yourself, in case you need them, consider setting up a 529 College Savings Plan for each of them. Look into your state-sponsored plan's expense level and performance history to see whether the added benefit of a tax deduction for your donations (up to a certain amount) makes it an attractive choice.

Once you have made sure you can cover your own necessities, you can open a 529 College Savings Account or some other college savings plan for your grandkids, in your name with your grandchild as the beneficiary. As long as any money withdrawn is used to pay for "approved" college expenses, interest and capital gains accumulate tax free.

If you need to, you can withdraw this money for your own use, but the withdrawal will be subject to taxes and a 10% penalty, unless it is used to pay your own college expenses. The money in a 529 account also is passed directly to the beneficiary upon your death, outside of your estate.

One other advantage of a 529 Plan for your grandkids is that, if you choose the vendor approved for your state, some or all of your contributions may be state-tax free. Go on line to www.savingforcollege.com to get information about your state's specific plan.

Finally, to get ahead of a heavy debt load, you might work with your grandchildren to select either a community college for the first two years (and then transfer to a four-year institution) or a college with a strong student assistance program. Doing so reduces the expense load from the beginning.

I don't have much money. Are there things to try as a way to make college more affordable when my son gets there?

MONEY TIP #48: Long before your son is ready for the big event, try to get him to excel academically to increase the likelihood of securing a scholarship, fellowship or grant to cover all or part of his college expenses. If that doesn't work, state schools and junior colleges are lower-priced options.

Hundreds of millions of dollars of scholarships, grants, tax credits, and benefits go unclaimed every year. Taking advantage of these funds can be complicated, but the payoff can be substantial over your son's college career.

- ▶ **Scholarships and Fellow**ships—According to the IRS, scholarship and fellowship money is tax-free if the student is a degree candidate at an eligible educational institution and the money is used for qualified education expenses.

  The best place to start your search for college scholarships is to look at those requiring residency in your own home state. They provide many of the most generous rewards. In addition, you may find valuable information on the following sites:
  1. www.scholarships.com/financial-aid/college-scholarships
  2. www.bigfuture.collegeboard.org/scholarship-search

- ▶ **Education Tax Credit**—Under certain circumstances, the IRS allows a credit on your tax return for college-related expenses through the American Opportunity Tax Credit or the Lifetime Learning Credit, depending upon your income level. Once you determine whether you qualify, then you can decide which tax credit would be better for you to take. Either credit can be taken for yourself, your spouse or your dependents. (You cannot claim either of these credits if your filing status is married filing separately, or if another person can claim an exemption for you or your son on his/her tax return.)

▸ **Student Loan Interest Deduction**—The IRS allows a deduction for interest on student loans, but there are income caps and other stipulations on this deduction. For you to take a deduction, you must be a signer on the loan documents and be responsible for its repayment.

▸ **Less Expensive Schools**—Your son can start his education at a less-expensive state school or a junior college and transfer at some point. He, then, can obtain the degree from a larger, more costly institution.

I am answering this question, in part, from personal experience. Right after I entered high school, my mother became a young widow, with five children. After that, because of our very limited resources, I absolutely needed tuition assistance to be able to further my education. Being awarded a scholarship was going to be an excellent way, if not the only way, for me to be able to go to college.

With lots of hard work and support, I was named valedictorian of my high-school class and received a four-year scholarship for undergraduate school. High performance there helped me secure a fellowship for my first graduate program. To date, I have completed one undergraduate program and four post-graduate programs, all of them with honors, and I never have had to pay out-of-pocket for any of my schooling. (The other three graduate programs were paid for by my employers.) I won't say this was an easy route or one that works for everybody, but I will say it worked for me and I didn't end up with vast student loans that I was burdened with trying to figure out how to repay.

CHAPTER 7

Common (and Not-so-Common) Money Scams

Keep What's Yours as Your Own

There are a lot of unscrupulous people who spend their time looking for folks who they think may either have money or have access to money. (This may be true whether or not you are employed, and whether you have cash at the moment.) These people stay up nights trying to invent new ways to swindle you out of your cash. Their scams come in many different forms and keep government agencies like the FBI, Consumer Financial Protection Bureau, Department of Justice, and many others busy, alerting consumers to the latest scams, teaching you how to protect yourself against them, and tracking down and prosecuting offenders.

Plain and simple—scams are schemes to con you out of your money. They can arrive by mail, phone call, text message, email, internet website, or a scammer on your doorstep.

Financial scams are ways of getting hold of your bank or investment details to steal money from your accounts. Some financial scam artists persuade you to invest in bogus deals involving shares of fake companies, or other inappropriate or non-existent investment products.

According to the Department of Justice, "...Identity theft and identity fraud are terms used to refer to all types of crime in which someone wrongfully obtains and uses another person's personal data in some way that involves fraud or deception, typically for economic gain."

Javelin Strategy & Research is a research-based advisory firm that helps its clients make informed decisions in a digital financial world. Javelin reported that in 2015, 15.4 million U.S. consumers were victims of identity theft and fraud in 2016, with losses totaling almost $16 billion—an increase of 16% over 2015. (The 2017 Equifax hacking scam has affected more than 143 million Americans, plus some overseas.)

The FBI cautions that the "over-40 crowd," especially seniors, is often targeted by con-artists for the following reasons:

▶ This group is most likely to have a sizable "nest egg."
▶ They are likely to be homeowners.
▶ Many have excellent credit.
▶ Most are too polite to hang up on strangers or close the door in their faces without listening to their spiel.

What are some of the red flags and scams I should look out for?

MONEY TIP #49: Stay alert and remain vigilant, constantly looking out for scammers. If it sounds too good to be true, it probably is.

Following is a description of some of the scams and tactics you might not have heard of. For more detailed information, go to www.usa.gov.

▶ Door-to-Door Scams:

Home Maintenance Services —You are given a cheap quote that requires an up-front deposit. The scammer either disappears with your money or raises the price and performs sub-par work.

Fake Energy-saving Gadget—You are sold a device that, when plugged in, the seller claims, will lower your energy bill by as much as 40%. The device does nothing to lower your bill.

Fake Green Deal Sales—You are told you are entitled to a large sum of money to fund Green Deal home improvements like insulation or a new boiler. You are then asked to pay an administrative fee to cover the cost of processing and shipping. After you pay the fee, you never see the scammer or your money again.

▶ "Too Good to Be True" Scams:

Fake Dates—You meet a person through a dating website and, before long, the person is asking you for money to cover real or imaginary bills. You send the requested money and, essentially, say goodbye to the potential suitor (and your money) unless he/she calls again with another monetary request.

Training Course Scam—You are the selected applicant for a high-salaried job that you apply for online. You then are told you must enroll in and pay for a training course of some kind to ensure you're ready for the new position. Of course, the job never materializes.

Tax Back—You get an email from a fraudulent group claiming you are entitled to a tax refund, but first you must confirm your personal details. They, then, use this information either to drain your bank account or create an identity for themselves using your information.

Pension Problems—You are contacted by a person, supposedly from The Pension Helpline, stating you are due a large bonus from the government because of pension underpayment. To get the bonus, you must first provide a host of identifying information, including your bank account number, and other personal data—just what's needed for identity theft.

Noise Rebatement—In this one, you are contacted by a supposed "government representative" advising you there may be monies owed to you because a former employer has been shut down due to noise. You are told you must pay a fee to get further information.

▸ **Scams Which Prey on Your Fears:**

Missed Payments—You are called by a person identified as a vendor or a credit card company representative. Because you are, supposedly, behind in your payments, an immediate catchup payment is demanded over the phone—either via credit card, money card, or a direct debit from your checking account.

Medical Emergency—You are called and told a loved one has been in an accident abroad. (You can hear someone screaming in agony in the background.) The caller requests that you send money immediately to cover their medical expenses. If this happens, contact your loved one to check on them, just to be sure they are ok.

Jury Duty Scam—You are called and told you did not show up for jury duty. You reply you never received a jury duty notice. (The truth is no such notice was ever sent.) The caller then asks you to verify your personal information so he/she can be sure they have the "right person." You are told a mistake has been made. The caller apologizes for the mix up, and hangs up. However, you now have given them all the data they need to create a false identity. (Like your bank and the IRS, a legitimate representative of the court system will never contact you via phone about a missed jury duty appearance.)

Tax Scam—You are called and told you owe the IRS and that a payment must be made immediately over the phone—via direct debit to your checking account or via credit card. You are also told if you do not pay, a U.S. Marshall will be at your door promptly to handcuff you and take you directly to jail. In a panic, you bite. By the time the call is over, the scammer has elicited enough personal data from you to create a fake identity, has your bank account or credit card number, and has succeeded in getting you to fork over some money.

▶ **Misleading (or Shady) Sales Tactics and Practices:**

Affinity Fraud—Scammers hire salespeople to target specific religious, ethnic, social or professional groups. Often, the salesperson is a member of the same group, thereby increasing his/her credibility with the target. Once trust is established and one person invests or makes a purchase, then the fraud is perpetrated on others in the same group who are then willing to consider becoming involved.

Churning—This occurs when a securities professional makes unnecessary trades or exchanges to generate commissions. This happens most often when your broker has your permission to make trades in your account without prior authorization.

Guaranteed Returns—You are promised a high return on a particular security product. You may be especially interested in this, as a way of quickly increasing the size of your retirement fund, which may be woefully underfunded. You should know it is illegal for legitimate brokers and financial advisors to guarantee a specific rate of return on a securities product.

▶ **Securities Fraud:**

Ponzi Schemes—These schemes consist of using the money obtained from new investors to pay early investors exorbitant returns. This scheme may work as long as the scammers continue to generate enough dollars from new clients to pay the promised returns to the earlier ones. When they can no longer attract new "bait," the whole scheme falls apart and, in most cases, investors lose money.

"Pump and Dump" Scams—Brokers and other unscrupulous people artificially inflate the value of a stock. When other investors start buying the stock, they sell or "dump" their stock, rendering the shares held by John-Q-Public virtually worthless.

▶ **Unregistered Activities:**

Investment Products—Scammers often try to sell unsuspecting consumers investment products that are not real and are not registered, as required by law. Before buying, check with local or federal regulators to confirm the legitimacy of the product.

Brokers—Brokers are required by law to be registered with federal regulators. Before entrusting your funds to them, confirm their legitimacy. This can be done by going to www.licensedbroker.gov.

▸ **Car-buying Scams:**

Internet Purchase Scam—Recently, the federal government has received a significant number of complaints from consumers who have "purchased" cars over the internet which they have paid for but have yet to receive. Payment is usually made via Western Union or wire transfer. At that point, the money is gone and the car is never received. In some cases, it never existed. Be very careful.

Used Car Scam—As money becomes tighter, more and more families than ever are buying used cars. Unfortunately, some law enforcement agencies report that vehicle identification number (VIN) cloning is on the rise. It targets used car buyers and the Better Business Bureau (BBB) advises car buyers to do research, or they could, unknowingly, buy a stolen car.

▸ **Mis-use of Better Business Trademark Scam**—The BBB has issued an international alert to warn about people misusing the BBB and BBB OnLine trademarks to extort money from online car shoppers.

In one case, the BBB received an inquiry from an online shopper who had searched for a car on cars.com. The shopper was sent an invoice by email from someone posing as an escrow service that displayed a cars.com and BBBOnLine banner, and listed several other BBB sites. The fraudulent email invoice contained claims the BBB and cars.com are trusted, neutral third parties. There was no affiliation.

▸ **Phony Escrow Company Scam**—The BBB has alerted online car shoppers that scammers pose as phony escrow services to defraud consumers out of thousands of dollars.

Internet thieves are now using escrow service fronts with some new twists to steal money and personal identities.

▸ **Charity Scam**—In a Charity Scam, money is solicited for fake charities. This often occurs after a natural disaster or high-profile crime, where funds are supposedly being collected to aid the victims, but are not. Often, the collector has no connection whatsoever to the victims.

I once was asked to teach a series of classes for a group that included spouses and parents of victims of 9/11. These beneficiaries were about to get large payouts from the U.S. government and the classes were an attempt at familiarizing the participants with basic money management skills so when they received their payouts, they would have an even better idea of how to handle their money and what to be on the lookout for.

In one class segment, I was talking about scams and how careful participants need to be because victims and beneficiaries' names were public information and had been printed in many news publications. One woman, whose son was on one of the planes, told a harrowing scam story that went as follows:

She went out to a local shopping mall to look for a dress to wear to her son's funeral. As she returned to her car, she encountered a woman in the parking lot who said her son was on one of the planes that had been crashed. She was asking for money for help with his funeral. The woman in my class, obviously touched by and interested in her story, compassionately asked the woman her son's name. Imagine her shock when the name the woman gave was the name of the son of the person she was talking to. My "student" replied, "Oh no he's not! _____ was **MY** son!!" The woman quickly turned and ran.

This one might have worked had the beggar not encountered the young man's real mother. Again, I urge you to proceed with caution any time you are asked for money or identifying information.

What are "advanced fee" scams?

MONEY TIP #50: "Advanced fee" scams are scams where you are required to put up money "in advance" to collect your prize. Never pay anyone for a prize you supposedly have won! It is probably a scam. If you can get the scammer's contact information, report both the scam and the scammer to the FBI.

"Advanced fee" scams trick you into paying money up front, with the promise of receiving goods, services, or money later on. But, none of these things ever arrive. Some examples are:

▶ You are offered huge fees in exchange for "helping" someone transfer money out of a country that's in trouble.

▶ Someone asks you to pay upfront fees for loans or credit cards that you don't receive.

▶ A buyer sends a check for something you're selling. The check is for more than the agreed price. You're then asked to return the difference. The buyer's check bounces, and you lose your money.

▶ A caller says you have won a prize in the Publisher's Clearing House Sweepstakes, but you need to send X number of Green Money cards from Walmart to pay the tax on your prize.

This one recently happened to someone I know. The caller swore my friend had won a car and asked whether she was near a Walmart. When she replied she was, he instructed her to get three $500 Green Money cards and call him when she got back home. When she questioned his legitimacy, he gave her his "ID number," her winning ticket number, his phone number, and swore he was legit.

She waited about 15 minutes and called the number he had given her. He answered the phone, "Hello." When she asked if this was Publisher's Clearing House, he hung up, abruptly. She waited another 15 minutes and called back. This time he answered with the name "Publisher's Clearing House." She hung up and filed a report with Publisher's Clearing House. They advised her they never ask for payment, and certainly would never do so over the phone.

Can you explain phishing, vishing and SMShing?

MONEY TIP #51: Each of these scams is characterized by a call, text or email from a person or entity pretending to be legitimate, and one whose name is likely to be familiar to you.

- ▶ In phishing, you get an **email, snail mail, or phone call** that claims to be from a familiar bank, vendor, or credit card company, asking you to confirm details of your account. These scams are designed to steal your money, or personal identity—and, then, your money.
- ▶ **In vishing,** you receive a **phone call** from someone who identifies himself as a bank employee, fraud investigation team member, or the police. They try to get financial information from you, like your credit or debit card details

(including PIN); bank account numbers; and your full name, date of birth, and address. This information is then used by the scammer to gain access to your finances or to get you to make payments into the scammer's account.

▸ SMShing (SMS phishing) is a type of phishing attack where **mobile phone users receive text messages** containing a website **hyperlink** which, if clicked, will download a Trojan horse onto the mobile phone. (A Trojan horse puts a lock on your phone (or computer) controlled by a crook who usually will not release it unless a ransom is paid.)

To be on the safe side, never provide your personal information to any caller you do not recognize or in response to any email, snail mail, or text request, even if it appears to be from a recognizable source. Contact the source directly using a phone number or email address you have looked up, not the one provided by the probable scammer.

I have a friend who almost lost her home through a foreclosure rescue scam. How do they work, and where can one go for help if you get caught in one of these scams?

MONEY TIP #52: The companies involved in foreclosure rescue scams claim they can assist homeowners facing foreclosure with options that allow them to keep their property, refinance or modify their existing mortgage. Usually, none of this is true. These companies gain your confidence and, in the end, also gain ownership of your property.

Examples of phony options proposed are:

▶ **Lease-back or Repurchase Scams**—In exchange for "temporarily" signing over your deed to them or a third party, the delinquent mortgage and other credit card debt are all paid off and the homeowner gets to remain in the home as a renter with an option to repurchase the home after the existing financial windstorm dies down. The problem is, after you sign over your home to the new lawful owner, the scammer then is able to do with the home as he/she likes. This may or may not include paying off the mortgage and credit card delinquencies, or allowing you to repurchase your home. If you can repurchase the home, it may be at an above-market price because the scammer knows you are desperate and will do almost anything to stay in your home.

▶ **Refinance Scams**—In this scam, the "mortgage broker" presents you with "foreclosure rescue" documents to sign that make the broker the temporary owner of your home, with a promise to re-sell the home to you. What you don't know is that by signing these documents, you are surrendering ownership of your home. (The loan documents are really deed transfer documents.) Often, by the time you discover the deception, it is too late to do anything about it. The home now belongs to the scammer and you may be forced out. Plus, you are still on the hook for the mortgage loans you originally signed for.

▶ **Internet and Phone Scams**—In this case, you are conned into applying for a loan over the internet or via phone. The caller, a scammer, obtains from you all of your vital information, thus creating the high probability of identity theft. Not only do you exchange completed documents, but also you likely have paid high fees and have been given the promise to save your house. In the end, both your identity has been stolen and your home is still in foreclosure because no payments have been paid to the real mortgage lender.

If you believe you are the victim of a foreclosure rescue scam, low-income families can get free legal service by contacting www. findlegalhelp.org. Also, a valuable resource available to help anyone who has been targeted is the FDIC's Foreclosure Assistance website at www.fdic.gov/foreclosureprevention.

Credit Score Description and Related Tips

The FICO score, the credit score used most frequently by lenders, is based on the five components listed below. FICO scores range from 300 to 850. The higher the score, the more creditworthy you are. Also, the higher your credit score, the lower the risk and, therefore, the lower the cost you likely will have to pay for credit.

The FICO score components and the relative weight each contributes to your overall score are:

- ▶ Your payment history—how timely you've been with payments. **35%**
- ▶ Your current total debt—how much you owe compared with your total available credit. **30%**
- ▶ Length of your credit history—how long a credit history you have. **15%**
- ▶ Types of credit you have outstanding—what mix of credit types you have. **10%**
- ▶ Your requests for new credit—whether you've recently taken on new credit or debt. **10%**

(If you apply for several credit cards within a short period of time, multiple inquiries will appear on your report. Most credit scores are not affected by multiple inquiries from auto, mortgage or student loan lenders within a short period of time.)

Here are a few credit score-related tips:

▸ According to Zogby International, one of the country's largest public opinion pollsters, a third of people who have pulled their credit reports have found errors in them. So, be sure to get a copy of your report from each credit bureau and read it! Getting an error fixed can raise your score by as much as 200 points, according to John Ulzheimer, president of consumer education at www. Credit.com.

▸ Paying your bills on time is the single most important contributor to a good credit score. "Even one late payment can reduce a 750+ credit score by 100 points," says Mr. Ulzheimer, "...but, if you catch up within 30 days, you may be able to get back on track." CNN reports that a payment that's more than 90 days late can cause damage to your credit score for years.

▸ If you feel you want to cancel some of your credit cards, don't cancel your oldest cards, since 15% of your credit score is determined by the length of your credit history.

▸ Many real estate agents and auto sales people tell clients that mortgage and car loan inquiries made within the most recent 30 days are not figured into the credit score calculation. All inquiries within a 14-day period before that count as a single inquiry.

▸ Pay off debt rather than move it around. Creditors can easily tell that an old balance has been "paid off" while a new account has been opened with an almost identical balance. They are not fooled.

Your FICO score makes a huge difference in the way lenders view you, and, consequently, the interest rate a potential lender is likely to charge you. So, know your score; correct any errors found on your credit report; and manage your score carefully.

For more information on credit scores and credit reports, go to the FICO website www.myfico.com/CreditEducation. (See Appendix C for contact information for the three major credit bureaus—Equifax, Experian and TransUnion.)

How to Create a Spending Plan

A spending plan (or budget) is simply an "at-a-glance look" at ALL of your expected income and expenses over a given period of time. The period covered should be for at least three months, but six months or more is preferred, since that gives you a better picture of your income and expenses over a longer timeframe and helps you remember to include the things that only happen once a year.

Making a budget requires a bit of patience but, if done accurately, will help you determine whether you can afford the lifestyle you want to live. Take the following steps:

1. Gather all documentation you have showing your income and expenses over the last six months, including:
   a) Check registers
   b) Bank statements
   c) Credit card statements
   d) Bill stubs for expenses like utilities, rent/mortgage, childcare
   e) Car payment book
   f) Mortgage or rent statements
   g) Pay stubs
   h) Tax returns

    i)   Other, such as tip records, gifts, tax refunds/payments, etc.

2. Make a separate pile containing the receipts/documentation for each expense category. This includes items such as:

    a)   Housing, including taxes and insurance

    b)   Transportation, including car payment, repairs and maintenance, gasoline, tags, insurance, road service, parking, registration, and vehicle personal property taxes

    c)   House maintenance

    d)   Food

    e)   Utilities, including electricity, gas, water, alarm monitoring, phones (cell and land lines), cable, trash and water

    f)   Entertainment

    g)   Vacation/travel

    h)   Laundry

    i)   Savings—regular, retirement, and emergency

    j)   Contributions/Tithes

    k)   Homeowner association fees

    l)   Medical, including co-pays and prescriptions

    m)   Insurance statements, including disability, life, and long-term care

    n)   Personal items, including hair and nails

    o)   Gifts, including Christmas, birthdays, anniversary, etc.

    p)   Clothing

    q)   Outstanding debts, including student loans and existing credit cards

    r)   Estimated federal and state taxes

    s)   Allowance

    t)   Miscellaneous

3. Add up the receipts for each expense category and divide by the number of months of receipts you have. (This gives you an initial estimate of your average monthly expense, by type.)

4. Make a list of all of your income sources, by month, including beginning checking account balance, net salaries, retirement income, child support, alimony, gifts, anticipated tax refunds, and any other income.

5. In a table, similar to the sample shown after these instructions, list all of the income and expenses from the steps above, in the appropriate months. By the time this is complete, essentially, every dime of income and expenses you expect to receive or pay should be reflected in the table.

6. Do the math, taking the following steps:
   a) Add up all of your income and expenses, by month.
   b) Subtract expenses from income, by month. (Some months may be positive; some may be negative.)
   c) Add all the monthly positives and negatives. If this total is negative, either find other sources of income or reduce expenses to make sure the total of the positives and negatives is zero or positive. This ensures your budget reflects a lifestyle you can afford.

Even after you have completed your spending plan for the chosen period, such a plan is not fixed forever. You must perform regular reviews and make changes to it as life circumstances change.

Changes to the spending plan may be required when there are new events like:

1. Salary adjustments
2. New tax schedules
3. New family goals

4.   A change in family status—marriage, divorce, separation
5.   New family members

Remember, your spending plan is not meant to shackle you. Instead, if done so it accurately and completely reflects your and your family's income and expenses, it can be your ticket to financial freedom.

SAMPLE BUDGET SPREADSHEET-PAGE 1

RESOURCES & EXPENSES / MONTH	JAN	FEB	MAR	APRIL	MAY	JUNE	JULY	TOTAL
CASH ON HAND	122							122
CHECKS FOR DEPOSIT	275							275
CKG ACCT BALANCE	1,169							1,169
CHG ACCT CREDITS	47 Macy's							47
MONIES OWED TO US	500 John T.							500
NET SALARIES:								
— YOU	2,500	2,500	2,500	2,500	2,500	2,500	2,500	17,500
— YOUR SPOUSE	3,200	3,200	3,200	3,200	3,200	3,200	3,200	22,400
TAX REFUND				360				360
GIFTS			100				50	150
INTEREST/DIVIDENDS	12	15	16	20	21	24	26	134
OTHER								0
TOTAL RESOURCES	7,825	5,715	5,816	6,080	5,721	5,724	5,776	**42,657**

SAMPLE BUDGET SPREADSHEET-PAGE 2

RESOURCES & EXPENSES / MONTH	JAN	FEB	MAR	APRIL	MAY	JUNE	JULY	TOTAL
TITHE (5%)	350	350	350	350	350	350	350	2,450
DONATIONS	50	50	50	50	50	50	50	350
SAVINGS	225	225	225	225	225	225	225	1,575
UTILITIES:								
ELECTRICITY	75	75	75	75	75	75	75	525
GAS								0
WATER	55		55		75		55	240
ALARM MONITORING	30	30	30	30	30	30	30	210
CABLE	35	35	35	35	35	35	35	245
PHONE SERVICES:								
CELL	65	65	65	65	65	65	65	0
LAND	30	30	30	30	30	30	30	0
CABLE	44	44	44	44	44	44	44	0
HOUSE-RELATED EXPENSES:								
1ST MORTGAGE	1,225	1,225	1,225	1,225	1,225	1,225	1,225	0
2ND MORTGAGE	560	560	560	560	560	560	560	0
TAXES	300	300	300	300	300	300	300	0
INSURANCE	75	75	75	75	75	75	75	0
LAWN CARE				40	40	50	40	170
HOUSE UPKEEP	100	100	100	100	100	100	100	700
NEWSPAPER	35	35	35	35	35	35	35	245
INSURANCES:								
AUTO			300			300		600
MEDICAL/COPAY	75	75	75	75	75	75	75	525
PRESCRIPTIONS	60	60	60	60	60	60	60	420
DENTAL/VISION	45	45	45	45	45	45	45	315
AUTO-RELATED:								
CAR PAYMENT (1)	222	222	222	222	222	222	222	1,554
CAR PAYMENT (2)	0	0	0	0	0	0	0	0
TAGS/LICENSE		155			123			278
ROAD SERVICE				65				65
REPAIRS-- CAR (1)			500					500
REPAIRS-- CAR (2)					600			600
GASOLINE	200	200	200	200	200	200	200	1,400
PARKING	175	175	175	175	175	175	175	1,225
SIRUS (both cars)				165				165

SAMPLE BUDGET SPREADSHEET-PAGE 3

RESOURCES & EXPENSES / MONTH	JAN	FEB	MAR	APRIL	MAY	JUNE	JULY	TOTAL
FOOD	300	300	300	300	300	300	300	2,100
LAUNDRY/DRY CLEANING	25			25				50
HAIR/HAIR PRODUCTS	10	85	10	85	10	83	10	293
ENTERTAINMENT	50	50	50	50	50	50	50	350
FAMILY MISC	100	100	100	100	100	100	100	700
TRAVEL						1,000		1,000
CONSUMER LOANS:								
CREDIT UNION	55	55	55	55	55	55	55	385
VISA	122	122	122	122	122	122	122	854
AMERICAN EXPRESS	81	81	81	81	81	81	81	567
MACY'S	44	44	44	44	44	44	44	308
STUDENT LOANS	285	285	285	285	285	285	285	1,995
CHILDCARE	400	400	400	400	400	400	400	2,800
TUITION	0							0
TRANSPORTATION	0							0
GIFTS:								
CHRISTMAS (HOLIDAY)							500	500
BIRTHDAYS		60		75			100	235
ALLOWANCE:								
YOU	100	100	100	100	100	100	100	700
YOUR SPOUSE	100	100	100	100	100	100	100	700
YOUR KIDS	60	60	60	60	60	60	60	420
CLOTHING (incl alterations)	250			250			250	0
OTHER	200			50			50	300
TOTAL OUTFLOW	5,813	5,573	6,138	6,028	6,121	6,706	6,278	42,657
MONTHLY PLUS/MINUS	2,012	142	-322	52	-400	-982	-502	0
CUMULATIVE BAL	2,012	2,154	1,832	1,884	1,484	502	0	

Helpful Resources

Financial Websites:

a) Rich Dad/Poor Dad: www.richdad.com

b) Social Security Administration: www.ssa.gov

c) Teaching kids about money: www2.cibc.com/smartsmart/ parent/TeachingThemAbout Money.html

d) Shows kids, teens and adults how to get on the road to financial freedom: www.creativewealthintl.org

e) Long-term-care Insurance: www.gefn.com; www.jhan-cock.com; www.ltcinsurance.com

Books for Adults:

a) *Rich Dad, Poor Dad*, Robert Kiyosaki

b) *Personal Finance for Dummies*, Eric Dyson

c) *The Money Book – A Smart Kid's Guide to Savvy Saving   and Spending*, Elaine Wyatt and Stan Hinden

d) *In the Black: The African-American Parent's Guide to   Raising Financially Responsible Children*, Fran Harris

e) *Smart Couples Finish Rich*, David Bach

f) *How Not To Go Broke At 102*, Adriane Berg
g) *7 Money Mantras For A Richer Life*, Michelle Singletary
h) *The Money Book for the Young, Fabulous & Broke,*
    Suze Orman
i) *The Ultimate Allowance Book*, Elisabeth Donati

Books for Kids:
a) *The Money Savvy Student*, Adam Carroll
b) *Loaded*, Sarah Newcomb
c) *What All Kids Should Know About Saving & Investing,*
    Rob Pevnick
d) *Alexander, Who Used to Be Rich Last Sunday,*
    Judith Viorst
e) *A Dollar for Penny*, Julie Glass

Credit Reporting Agencies:
a) Equifax:
    P.O. Box 740241
    Atlanta, GA 30374
    1-800-685-1111
    www.equifax.com
b) Experian:
    P.O. Box 2002
    Allen, Texas 75013
    1-888-567-8688
    www.Experian.com
c) TransUnion Corporation:
    P.O. Box 390 Chester, PA 19022
    1-800-916-8800
    www.transunion.com

Other:

a) Federal Trade Commission
CRC-240 Washington, D.C. 20580
www.ftc.gov
You can write to this agency if documented evidence of an error is not acted upon by each credit bureau within 30 days. They also enforce credit laws and provide free information.

b) Fair Credit Reporting Act
1-877-382-4357
www.ftc.gov/os/ststutes/frca.html
This act gives you the right to know what information is being distributed about you by credit reporting agencies.

c) National Foundation for Credit Counseling–www.nfcc.org
This foundation will help you find a professional non-profit credit counseling service.

d) Consumer Credit Counseling Service
www.cccsf.org
This service will advise you how to clear up a bad credit report.

e) FICO
www.myfico.com
Provides information about credit reports.

f) GMAC Financial Services
1-800-327-6278
www.SmartEdgeByGMAC.com
This site provides educational information on credit and budgeting; automobile financing; mortgages; and banking and insurance.

g) Websites for Kids:
www.kidsenseonline.com, www.finishrich.com, www
coolbank.com, www.kidsource.com, www.bigchange.
com, www.kipplinger.com/kids

h) Financial Planners:
1-800-322-4237
www.fpanet.com
This site allows you to search for names of certified financial planners, by zip code.

i) Junk Mail / Fraud:
www.dmachoice.org
Direct Marketing Association consumer opt-out service -
to reduce junk mail
1-888-567-8688 or www.opoutprescreen.com
consumer credit reporting agency opt-out service — to
stop credit card and insurance offers
www.donotcall.gov or 1-888-382-1222
National Do Not Call Registry

j) Budget Software:
www.mint.com
www.YouNeedABudget.com
HomeBudget with Sync (from www.Anishu.com
Available at App Store and Google Play
VisualBudget (from www.kiwiobjects.com)
Available at App Store and Google Play
MoneyWiz Personal Finance (from www.Wiz.money.com)
Available at App Store and Google Play

Index

About the Author

PATRICIA DAVIS, B.S., M.B.A., M.S. is a former corporate financial management executive. She uses her extensive financial expertise to conduct seminars, nationwide, on the topic of Financial Literacy—a subject about which she is passionate. A veteran author, speaker, and educator, she also provides personal financial counseling to individuals (and couples) at all income levels with a special emphasis on under-served populations. Ms. Davis is the Managing Director of Davis Financial Services and is the Executive Director of Money Matters, Inc., a 501 C (3) non-profit corporation. Both provide financial literacy education and training, and financial counseling. Also, she is a licensed provider of Camp Millionaire, a financial literacy education program for kids, teens, and adults.

Ms. Davis, a native of Washington, D.C., received a B.S. in mathematics and statistics, *cum laude*, from Howard University. She finished near the top of her M.B.A. class at Stanford University and became the first minority in the Business School's history to graduate with honors. Ms. Davis also has a Master of Science degree in Personal Financial Planning from Golden Gate University where she received her class' Top Student Award. She graduated, *with distinction*, from the Stonier Graduate School of Banking at Georgetown University. Ms. Davis is a former White House Fellow and served as Special Assistant to the Secretary of Labor. She was one of two Maryland state representatives on the Taxpayer Advocacy Panel, an Internal Revenue Service citizens advocacy group that focuses on improving IRS responsiveness to taxpayer needs. She is a recipient of Golden Gate University's Alumni Community Service Award in acknowledgement of her work in providing financial literacy to underserved populations, including students, teens, welfare-to-work participants, federal employees, and seniors.

Ms. Davis is the author of *Mimi, Money and Me--101 Realities About Money Daddy Never Taught Me but Mama Always Knew*, endorsed by the *Washington Post*'s financial columnist, Michelle Singletary, as "... one of the best books to give if you want to give the gift of financial power in the form of a good book." It is a wide-ranging, practical, easy-to-read, entertaining money management primer that discusses the realities associated with 101 money-related myths, misunderstandings, and misconceptions. *Mimi, Money and Me* is written to be a valuable resource for all ages to help put the reader squarely on the road to financial freedom.

Her second book, *Money Secrets for the Sandwich Generation (Squeezed in the Financial Middle)*, is written for those caring for both aging parents/grandparents and adult/minor children. It offers specific steps on how to care for yourself first, as well as for the other two sides of the "sandwich," and provides real-life examples of challenges and solutions that work.

Ms. Davis is married, is a marathoner, and travels extensively.

Schedule of Services

Davis Financial Services

www.yourmoneywiz.com

- ▸ Financial literacy seminars / workshops
- ▸ Public Speaking
- ▸ Camp Millionaire
- ▸ Individual / couples financial counseling
- ▸ Goal-setting seminars
- ▸ Spending plan development
- ▸ Income tax planning
- ▸ Retirement planning

www.ingramcontent.com/pod-product-compliance
Lightning Source LLC
Chambersburg PA
CBHW060317220326
41598CB00027B/4355